DAYS OF WINE AND SUSHI

AN ENGLISH PERSPECTIVE ON JAPAN

Marcus Grant

authorHOUSE™

1663 LIBERTY DRIVE, SUITE 200
BLOOMINGTON, INDIANA 47403
(800) 839-8640
WWW.AUTHORHOUSE.COM

First published by AuthorHouse 11/09/05

ISBN: 1-4208-8864-1 (sc)

Printed in the United States of America
Bloomington, Indiana

This book is printed on acid-free paper.

To Boof

ACKNOWLEDGEMENTS

First of all I must thank my wife and children for allowing me to go to Japan in the first place. This was not an easy decision to make for any of us, but it was far easier for me than it was for them! I must also thank them for having me back!

Thanks also to:

Nonaka Michihiro for becoming my first Japanese friend.
Ayu *tenchō* for making me feel so welcome and a little bit special.
Rohan Charlton and Cameron Phipps for being such good mates.
The lady volunteers who tried so patiently to teach me Japanese.
Tsuboi Kiyoyasu, Ishikawa Minoru, Wada Saeko and Hosoe Tamiki for being such loyal and enthusiastic students.
Matsui Hikō for introducing me to the mysteries of *saké* brewing.
Professor Kato Tomohiro for saving my life.
Masta and Mama at the pub '*teppen*' for their encouragement and kind gifts.
The nameless, homeless guy at the station for putting life into perspective.
Mr Leaflet for being so openly rude; it made a pleasant change!
Eileen, Bill and Declan at the *Stag's Head* in

Portslade Old Village for their constructive criticism and helpful comments.
The singer/songwriter Nagabuchi Tsuyoshi for writing *Himawari*.
Kuwano Junko for teaching me to sing it, for introducing me to *karaoke* and for a multitude of other kindnesses.

To them all, and to the countless others who made my life in Japan so memorable:

dōmo arigatō gozaimashita

CONTENTS

FOREWORD

I am not really sure what sort of book this is. It is not an autobiography, because only well-known people write those. It is not a travelogue, because I only travelled around the central region of Japan.

It isn't a sociological thesis, but there are elements of some sort of sociological musings (whatever sociology is, I never really found out!) and it isn't a history of Japan but there are references to historical events and characters. After all, I lived in the cradle of modern Japanese history and was surrounded by it in terms of natural features and buildings.

It is not particularly analytical, nor is it purely descriptive. It is not an instruction manual on how to live in Japan, but it does contain a few pointers for anyone thinking of spending some time teaching English there, or indeed for anyone thinking of just visiting the country.

What it *is* meant to be is a record of a couple of years spent working in Japan. I went to that country with no preconceptions; I had lived long enough in other countries to be dismissive of stereotypes, so I didn't really know what to expect. Indeed I was most surprised, on my first visit, to discover that they drive on the left. I had never known that, or even given the matter any thought.

Almost every day was an eye opener which added a new dimension, a new quality, to what had been a pretty jaded view of life pre-Japan (mainly work-related!)

This book is, above all, meant to be a tribute to the many warm-hearted and welcoming people whom I met and it is meant to serve as a fond memory of an extraordinary, life-enhancing period of my life. I blow a few trumpets, thump a few tubs and my tongue may sometimes brush fleetingly against my cheek, but basically I write with simple honesty and good humour. All I wish to do is to share those memories with other people.

I have used many Japanese words and phrases in these pages and I have not supplied a glossary. Nor have I used capital letters when writing such terms, except for proper nouns. I have, however, taken care to explain these terms, either in the text or in the form of footnotes. I have also kept to the Japanese convention of writing people's names family name first; it seems more natural to me.

nihon e yōkoso

Welcome to Japan

Marcus Grant
2005

CHAPTER 1

GIFU SHI

I didn't choose Gifu, it chose me. Having taken the view that I had wasted almost thirty years of my life trying to din the French and German languages into the mainly unreceptive heads of British teenagers, I took a TESOL course and I applied for jobs in Japan. After a period of waiting, an e-mail winged it's way to my PC offering possible employment in a small, independent school of English in Gifu city in Gifu Prefecture in the Chubu region of the island of Honshu. In other words, if you imagine the main island of Japan to be a banana, Gifu is bang in the middle of the banana.

So why does a family man in his fifties suddenly up sticks and leave the wife and kids behind to seek a new career in Japan? The answer is quite simple, really. I have, for much of my life, been attracted to the idea of Japan. I had trained in judo and karate, all the training was in the Japanese language, language is the expression of a nation's culture, so I attempted to study the language in more depth. Hmm, yes, well it doesn't work without a good teacher but, having mastered two European languages, I thought I could breeze through Japanese with little trouble. I was mistaken.

The only solution, for me, was to go there; I had the blessing of my family, all young adults either at, having completed or waiting to go to university or college – 'Hey, Dad, you've got a job in Japan. You must do it!' - and my long-suffering wife, whose tolerance and understanding know no bounds, said, 'Yes, darling, please bugger off for a bit!' So bugger off I did and fate took me to Gifu.

Gifu was given its name in the sixteenth century by the feudal lord Ōda Nobunaga, who had a castle built on a small mountain called Mount Kinka which overlooks the Nagara River, one of three rivers which converge to join the Pacific Ocean at the head of Ise Bay close to the port of Nagoya.

The city stands on a vast central plain[1] ringed on three sides by not so much mountains as big pointy hills, although Mount Ibuki, being roughly one third the height of Mount Fuji, is an impressively beautiful landmark, particularly in winter when its snow-capped peak stands starkly outlined against an aquamarine sky.

By Japanese standards Gifu is a small city, a mere 410,000 souls, and so is regarded by the sophisticated inhabitants of nearby Nagoya (pop. 4,000,000 and which claims to be the fourth largest city in Japan) as a bit of a rural backwater full of country bumpkins. It even has trams!

The good people of Nagoya have got it wrong, Gifu is a vibrant modern city with several universities (including one for women only) a medical school, many hospitals with nationally and internationally eminent specialists, a wonderful Prefectural library

---

[1] Most of the population of Japan lives on the flat bits. It can be a bit of a squeeze!

with every state-of-the-art facility and a variety of museums.

It has attractive covered shopping malls where you can escape from the fierce heat of the sun or from the torrential rain, luxury hotels, restaurants of every description, and a magnificent JR[2] railway station where you can eat in any number of restaurants and cafés, have a hot bath, learn Japanese or calligraphy or computer skills and buy designer clothes and jewellery. You can also catch a train there.

There is, I understand, a raunchy nightlife if you have a yen for that sort of thing. You need buckets of yen, in fact! There is a cluster of 'love hotels' on the outskirts where couples may enjoy their furtive trysts and there is a big modern Cultural Centre with a large theatre where I once watched a delightful concert of guitar and mandolin music being performed by High School students. About a hundred of them!

Every July the city is host to the biggest firework display in Japan and every September the Gifu *matsuri*, festival, takes place. This is a colourful occasion when hundreds of proud citizens parade through the main streets in costumes, and in a sequence, which reflect the progress of the city from a state of war to an era of peace.

Thus heavily armed *samurai*, followed by their mounted warlords, one of whom is, of course, Oda

---

[2] Japan Railways. This used to be nationalised, but it now
    consists of four private companies.

Nobunaga, stage a mock battle which is eventually succeeded by dozens of identically kimono clad ladies who perform a seemingly endless, synchronised dance of peace. This spectacular manoeuvre would swell the chest of any RSM.[3]

Above all, Gifu is *genki*, which is rather like saying it has *chutzpa*. And you can get around it very easily by bicycle. Just beware of the tramlines! Litter bins are few and far between, but then so is litter, and the pavements are free of chewing gum. There are, however, plenty of public ashtrays. As well as being a shopper's paradise, Japan is a smokers' paradise and there are cigarette machines everywhere you care to look.[4] Even my local chemist's shop sold fags.

Upon my arrival in Gifu city I occupied a spartan, two-roomed flat in a ward called Kashima-chō. There was a spare bicycle available, and so I took advantage of this wonderful facility and explored my environs. The city centre was a mere fifteen minutes ride away and the route took me along a busy, wide thoroughfare called the Gifu *tōzaidori*, the east-west road, which was bounded by a mixture of low-rise modern apartment blocks, offices, shops and eateries and the ten-storey municipal hospital, the *shimin byōin*.

---

[3] Regimental Sergeant Major, for any younger reader who has no idea who really runs the British Army.

[4] These machines automatically close down between the hours of 11pm and 5am to prevent the under-twenties from purchasing the evil weed. I'm not sure how that actually works in practice!

All I was able to focus upon, however, was the horrible tangle of criss-crossing, substantial power lines, transformers and junction boxes which blight every city, town and village in the country, except centres of historical and World Heritage interest such as the more photogenic parts of the very ancient capital, Nara.

Yes, I <u>know</u> that we all entirely depend upon electricity for our survival, but the gas and water supplies are buried beneath the streets, so why not electricity? I suppose that, being prone to the disruption caused by the occasional unannounced earthquake, it is easier to re-establish an above-ground supply grid. It is, nevertheless, an ugly visual intrusion.

What Gifu, along with all the other towns and cities that I visited, <u>is</u> very good at is provision for disabled people.

Street crossings, shop entrances, even pedestrian subways are mainly wheelchair friendly, and the 'yellow brick road', a strip of ribbed, yellow-painted concrete paving slabs, is a guide for the visually-impaired along all main streets, staircases, footbridges, train and underground station concourses and platforms, and shopping malls.

Pelican-crossings at all junctions have a different 'bleep' for north-south (cuckoo, cuckoo) and east-west (cheep, cheep) and I have even crossed the road at one where a female voice announced when the signal had turned green. Oddly the traffic lights, even though they display green, are referred to as being *ao*, blue. The word for 'green', *midori*, is normally only applied to the natural green of trees and all other growing plants.

*****

Gifu is also steeped in history and tradition. In common with anywhere else in Japan you can turn a corner and encounter a shrine, a stall selling fried octopus in batter, a commemorative stone recalling an event or personality of local history in finely-chiselled *kanji*[5], a beautifully maintained garden or park, or even a rice field.

Two-storey wooden houses rub shoulders with modern high-rises, the kimono sits comfortably alongside the business suit, the abacus is sometimes used in preference to the cash register, and the deferential bow is a constant reminder of the innate sense of hierarchy that permeates Japanese society.

A visit to the castle atop Mount Kinka, either by the 'Ropeway' (cable car) or up the winding, seemingly endless flight of steps, affords views southwards to the tower blocks of Nagoya, and westwards to Mount Ibuki which broods over the battlefield of Sekigahara.

It was here, in October1600, that Tokugawa Ieyasu defeated Ishida Mitsunari in one of the bloodiest military encounters in Japanese history, involving the largest armies ever seen in that country, and thus ensured his family's position as absolute rulers of Japan until 1868.

---

[5]   Chinese characters

History and tradition in the city of Gifu, however, find their most colourful expression in the ancient skill of cormorant fishing, *ukai*, between May and October on the Nagara River. This craft is roughly 1300 years old and is a spectacular and effective method of catching a small, sweet-fleshed fish called *ayu.*

Sea cormorants, patiently and lovingly trained for several years, are harnessed in groups of about six birds. Under the guidance of the fishing master, they swallow the *ayu* which are attracted by the light from a blazing pinewood fire hanging in an iron basket which dangles above the prow of the hand-poled fishing boat. The fish are then regurgitated into the hull and the cormorants pop back into the river for another go.

There are six fishing boats which progress in line abreast to drive the fish to shallower water. This helps the cormorants and gives a clearer view to the flotilla of river-borne spectators. They, after being entertained by an informative talk (with video) about the history of *ukai* and how the birds are trained, and by musicians, dancers and fireworks, relax with their *bentō*[6] boxes in the covered spectator punts. *Sotto voce,*[7] they urge on the advancing line of fire from the proximity of the

---

[6] Packed meal of mainly rice, fish and pickles - there's a wide variety at various prices.

[7] Making loud noises after the end of the firework display is frowned upon. It can distract the birds

river bank. The *ayu* are sold to restaurants, hotels, *ryokan*[8] and *bentō* compilers, and, of course, they are fed to the deserving cormorants.

In 1886 an American artist by the name of John La Farge spent several months travelling around Japan. He describes the cormorant fishing in his book 'An Artist's Letters From Japan' and compares the skill of the fishing master to that of the driver of a four-in-hand. Nothing, it seems, has changed in the intervening years, even down to the traditional dress of the fishermen, with the exception that in La Farge's day there were no spectator boats, just the urgent business of fishing.

Gifu city is also the home of the largest *papier-mâché* statue of Buddha in Japan. The statue is housed in a palatial building near the foot of Mount Kinka close to the Nagara River. Paper is the basis of the ancient traditional crafts in the city, namely the making of paper lanterns and umbrellas. These charming items are still produced today, in particular the lanterns, *chōchin*, which are specially made for festivals in Gifu and elsewhere.

This, then, was the area in which I would live and work for the next couple of years, and which I would come to know, love, and call home.

*****

Well, the job with the small, independent school of English didn't work out, so I had two choices: (a) coming back home with egg on my face, or

---

[8] Traditional Japanese inn

(b) getting a job with another establishment. The second option succeeded, I secured a teaching post with a large language institute which had schools all over the Chubu region, and I moved into an unfurnished studio flat in the west side of the city. This sounds simple enough, but we are talking Japan here. Here is some essential advice about getting a flat:

Step 1. Go to City Hall and get a certificate of alien registration (*gaikokujin kādo*). You need a couple of passport photos, an address in Japan (temporary will do) and it is essential to have a referee, such as a potential employer. You don't need any other visa beyond the 90-day visa that is issued by immigration upon entry into Japan. You will be given a specific date upon which you may collect your card. It is plastic, credit card sized and renewable after one year. Thereafter it is valid for a number of years and it means you don't have to carry your passport around with you.

Step 2. Take your *gaijin kādo* and your passport to a bank and open an account. *Gaijin* is short for *gaikokujin* and isn't very polite. There will be more about this later. Oh, yes, lots more, I promise you! When you open an account you will have the option of supplying a specimen signature or of using a personal seal, an *inkan*. The signature is more secure (although there are hundreds of different *inkan*) but when you come to sign any document there is very little room for a signature, all documents have a small circle for you to stamp with your seal. Getting a bank account is quick and easy and you can open one with as little as one yen. It takes a couple of weeks for your plastic to arrive. Until it does you have to go in person with your passbook to withdraw cash. They don't use cheque books.

Step 3. Apply for a certificate of eligibility... your potential employer may do this on your behalf, if not, fill in the application form yourself, but expect a delay while someone translates it into Japanese for you. I was fortunate in having the most efficient Personnel Lady in the whole of Japan who did the lot... all I had to do was sign the form.

Step 4. When your certificate of eligibility arrives take it to the nearest immigration office and apply for a visa. Get there before the office opens unless you are really into queuing. You will be given a date upon which your visa will be issued. I had thought of myself as just a humble teacher, so imagine my delight when both my certificate and my eventual visa proclaimed me to be a 'Specialist in Humanities and International Services'. It was akin to receiving a Birthday Honour and a Nobel Prize in the same year!

Step 5. Deflate ego, return to the immigration office first thing (queues, remember) on the appointed date and obtain your visa for a fee of 4,000 yen. Do not forget to obtain a multiple re-entry visa at the same time. There goes another 6,000 yen. Actually it doesn't work out all that expensive, given that both visas are valid for three years, and compared with the cost of a visa for the UK it is virtually given away! The multiple re-entry visa is essential if you wish to visit any other country and not lose your work permit upon your return to Japan. And that could be a problem.

Step 6. Sign contract with employer. The employer could be your guarantor...or not. A colleague of mine left the company and joined another one. His new employer would not act as his guarantor, but, fortunately for him, his girlfriend sponsored him. Be sure to get a guarantor before even thinking of finding a place of your own. No sponsor, no flat, and if you change your job, make sure that the new outfit will act as your guarantor, otherwise you are out in the street!

Step 7. Find a flat at a letting agency (Mini-Mini is pretty good in my experience) show all your documentation, especially your contract of employment, sign an agreement, pay the administration fees and move in. You pay the rent by automatic transfer at a cash point. Return to City Hall and register your change of address. Your *gaijin ka-do* will be amended to include the new information. If you don't register the change you'll never get a phone! I found that getting a mobile phone was almost as difficult as obtaining membership of the MCC is reputed to be. A further complication is that whatever phone company you choose it won't provide a facility for international calls, you have to go elsewhere to get that. Oh, and don't forget to give your new address to the bank.

With the exception of Steps 3 and 6, all of the above is done in Japanese! *gambatte kudasai!*[9]

*****

So, having completed Steps 6 and 7, and having arranged for the gas and electricity to be turned on, burdened with two suitcases, a briefcase, a hastily bought mat to sleep on and a single gas ring to cook on, I moved from the grubby flat[10] provided by the independent school into a flat that I had chosen for myself in the next city ward, about a five-minute walk away. Why so close? Well, for one thing it was cheap, the rent was the equivalent of about £200 per month, and after only one month in Gifu, that area of the city was really all I knew about the place.

There was a view of Mount Kinka from the balcony and a distant view of Mount Ibuki from the entrance. The most important consideration, however, was proximity to a railway station as I was scheduled to teach in three different schools, two of which were about a 10 - 15 minute train ride

---

[9]   Good luck! In my case I did all the transactions in a *mélange* of gibberish and sign language!

[10]   It was grubby when I moved *in*, honest!

away. Nishi Gifu[11] station was within a casual stroll[12] from my smart new flat, there was a coffee shop opposite where one could get a pretty substantial breakfast for under £2 and I knew there was a decent supermarket nearby, so there you have it, 'Bye-bye Kashima-chō, Hello Nishinoshō'.

****

---

[11] West Gifu
[12] It really is inadvisable to rush anywhere in the oppressive heat and humidity of a Japanese summer, especially in the Nagoya area, which can be the hottest region in Japan.

CHAPTER 2

NISHINOSHŌ

Nishinoshō is difficult to categorize as a suburb, if that indeed is what it is. It is largely residential with a mix of private housing and modestly proportioned apartment blocks, but there are small businesses (timber merchants, distributors, kitchen and bathroom fitters). There are some shops such as a convenience store, a pharmacy and Sanshin supermarket, a plethora of eating houses, notably *ramen-ya*[1], coffee shops, *shintō* shrines, vegetable plots and, above all, rice field upon rice field, some so small as to be squeezed in between buildings.

There was even a charming little hanging vineyard diagonally across from my flat. The rice fields are bordered by concrete irrigation channels about three feet deep and, as there is no protective wall between the road and the ditch, anyone walking or cycling under the influence of alcohol could be in for a muddy bath.

The ward is sliced in half by a major thoroughfare known as the Gifu Beltway which guides the traffic jams towards Nagoya and which I had to cross in order reach to the supermarket, the pharmacy, the ciggy machine or the pub. The city fathers had kindly provided a pedestrian subway, as well as a pelican crossing, and I had the impression that this was for my sole benefit, as, in all the time I

---

[1]   Chinese noodle bars, i.e. the noodles are Chinese, not the staff.

was living in Nishinoshō, I never met anyone else when using it.

Although my flat was only yards from the Beltway, I couldn't hear the traffic when I closed the door between my one all-purpose room and the kitchen/entrance area, but there were plenty other sources of noise, beginning with the 'The Men who Shout'.

'The Men who Shout' were employees of a small maintenance company whose HQ was on the ground floor, directly underneath my flat. Each morning these worthy and industrious men would foregather and in a bonding, mutually encouraging sort of way, would shout the company mantra at the tops of their voices.

Then, wearing their smart Lovat green working uniforms, they leapt into their smart white vans with gleaming aluminium ladders on the roofs, and zoomed off to perform their allotted tasks. They left their kimono-clad lady boss to the onerous tasks of drinking the coffee that the waitress from the coffee-shop opposite brought daily and taking phone-calls. 'The Men who Shout' gracefully left the floor to 'The Kids who Bash'"

'The Kids who Bash' were the entire student body of the nearby kindergarten. At every opportunity (i.e. when it wasn't raining) these tots would be paraded into the playground, issued drums and cymbals, and would be drilled into accompanying the slowest and most inept keyboard player in the Far East. In spring 2003 the favourite tune was 'When the Saints go Marching In'. It went something like this:

'Ooooooooh........whe..e..en....the.....Sai..ai..nts'

BOOM! BANG! BOOM BANGER BANGER BANG, BOOM BANGER BANGER CRASH CRASH!

'Go...oh....mar....ar...ching....i..i..in'

BOOM BOOM BANG BANG CRASH BANG BOOM! BOOM BANGER BANGER CRASH BANG.

In autumn 2002 the number one hit was 'Auld Lang Syne'. Until then I had been totally unaware that Auld Lang Syne has about thirty-seven verses. Fortunately 'The Clock that Invents Time' announced a pause in this soothing and productive activity.

'The Clock that Invents Time' was a public chime, an electronic replica of Big Ben, which announced the quarters during the hours of daylight. It was, mercifully, switched off at night. This chime would have been a useful pointer to the day's progress had there not been, about a kilometre away, an identical chime which firmly established its independence by Big Benning approximately ten minutes later than its neighbour.

My flat was roughly equidistant between the two. Consequently one had no idea of the time without reference to a timepiece. I always set my watch to the time displayed by JR station clocks, they are unerringly accurate and the trains run strictly on time unless delayed by an accident or a suicide.

It happens, as a later chapter will confirm *shōgunai wa!*[2]

At various times during the day would come the *tōfu*[3] seller who announced his approach by blowing a hunting horn. He was a very old, weather-beaten chap who looked like a walnut and who pedalled his bike and sidecar around Nishinoshō and adjacent wards in all weather conditions. He had a mighty pair of lungs, to judge by the frequency and energy of his horn-blowing which appeared to happen every few seconds. I only saw him make a sale on about three occasions.

Periodically there would be the waste-paper-and-cardboard truck which played a mindless jingle at such a loud volume that you could hear its tortured, distorted appeal streets away. Even louder were the loudspeaker vans that prowled the streets in convoy at election time. It seemed as if all the different political parties involved were playing follow-my-leader around the same circuit and their bellowed entreaties would rapidly succeed each other at window-rattling frequencies:

Candidate: '*Thank you very much, thank you very much. Soon we have big erections. Prease boat. Prease enjoy happy erections, they will bling briss to your rife.*'

Lorries have a built-in recorded female voice that supplements the indicators by loudly proclaiming whether the vehicle is turning left or right. Any

---

[2]   That's life!
[3]   Bean curd.

public service vehicle driver, from minibus upwards, appears to be incapable of reversing without the aid of someone blowing the Japanese equivalent of the Acme Thunderer whistle (*akumi dandara* perhaps?). In the road overlooked by my balcony there was a series of iron inspection covers. One didn't fit properly and every time it was driven or cycled over, it would go CLONK CLONK.....BONK BONK.

Then there was the dog! This wretched beast was tethered in the driveway of the spacious house in which it dwelt and amused itself by barking at ten-second intervals during the hours it spent alone outside, which meant most of the day. The pattern was always the same..ARF ARF (pause) ARF ARF ARF. Nobody complained, because complaining is very embarrassing to Japanese people, but they did moan about it to each other in the coffee shop.

They moaned about everything in the coffee-shop, probably because it had a large, yellow plastic canopy outside which plunged the interior into permanent gloom. In place of real lives, they had fertile imaginations, especially the owner, a small, rotund man called Masaharu, the top of whose head I never saw as he always wore a headscarf sort of thing. He could have been bald, I suppose, and he was only thirtyish. Anyway, I referred to him as 'Hankyhead'.

He spent a large proportion of his working day standing on the corner outside the shop, from where he had a field of vision that encompassed four little streets. I had a casual visitor one day, a female student of mine who was returning a book that I had lent her. 'Congratulations, *sensei*,' said Hankyhead, 'you have a woman. I saw her car. I can see everything from here.' 'Great,' said I, 'I had a shit this morning. Did you see that?'

****

My little flat was not exactly an oasis of peace and quiet either. The balcony is not a place for relaxing on, it is where you keep the washing machine and hang out your washing (but not smalls, I noticed!) or aired your *futon* and duvet. Not having a washing machine, I made my balcony into a pleasant little area with flowers in planting trays and hanging baskets, and a folding canvas chair in which I could sit and enjoy the morning sunshine and the view of Mount Kinka in the distance. In the evenings, on those days when I wasn't at work, I would relax and watch the local bats darting about.

I had reckoned without *taijitsu*. This was the nickname that I had bestowed upon my next-door-neighbour's washing machine, and is an amalgamation of the first syllables of the Japanese words for typhoon-*taifu*, earthquake-*jishin* and tidal-wave-*tsunami*.

The last component is particularly apposite, as this infernal appliance would generously dispense soapy water all over my balcony every time it was used, which was most days around either 11pm or 5am.

These times roughly coincided with the activities of 'The Whore Next Door'. This was my other next-door-neighbour who, I decided shortly after moving in, was a sex-worker. I think my assessment was justified as she would regularly wake me up in the small hours by loudly engaging in patently salacious phone calls which involved much throaty laughter and peculiar slurping noises.

After a couple of hours of this, round about 3am, she would slam her door shut and tap-tap her high-heeled way down the echoing concrete stairwell to a waiting taxi and, one assumes, a couple of hours of bliss, rapture and simulated orgasms. All would be calm again until the man in the flat above mine woke up. He had a seemingly incurable, hacking cough, and as it is unheard of to wear shoes indoors in Japan, I guessed this guy wore hobnailed socks.

To escape from all this racket I would occasionally pop into the *izakaya* just across the main road. This was a chain-pub delightfully named *yoro no taki*, 'The Waterfall of Yoro.' Yoro is a slightly disappointing village with no real focal point some twenty miles away, but which does, indeed, boast a magnificent waterfall issuing from a crack high up in a densely wooded big pointy hill. The din was phenomenal.

The entire staff, about seven of them, would bellow a welcoming *irrashaimase*[4] and your order would be promptly taken. Pubs are not just places for drinking in, the Japanese always order

[4]   Welcome, come in.

food to accompany their booze and their high-decibel conversation which usually drowns out the background music. When the dishes were ready the cooks behind the open counter would scream something like "The *yaki soba*'s ready" and the serving staff would noisily acknowledge this fact.

When customers left, a chorus of *itte'rasshai*[5] would reverberate in a friendly farewell which dislodged your ear wax. But I did like this place, it is where I made my first Japanese friends and the staff made a real fuss of me, especially the manageress, Ayu *tenchō*, and the cook, Ogawa *kun*.

Not all the noise was irritating. I found few things more relaxing than walking from the station in the warm spring and summer air of a late evening, past rice-fields where frogs entertained each other with their constant repertoire of croaking and whistling. Or in the daytime sitting in a park or just walking along past trees where hundreds of crickets chirped and where, now and then, a cicada would astonish one by the loudness of its rasping 'GLARK!' It's a shame that the cicadas all seem to die at the same time and streets, even in cities, become a crunchy carpet of corpses.

*****

Nishinoshō is bordered to the South by the JR Tōkaidō line under which one walks or cycles via

---

[5] Please come back.

a choice of three pedestrian underpasses, two on the eastern side, one on the western side, (cyclists are pedestrians with wheels) or, of course, under which one drives along the Beltway. The city ward beyond the railway line contains everything one could possibly want: another supermarket, another pub, a large DIY store with a small garden centre, a fancy goods store, a bedding centre, men's and women's outfitters, hairdressers, dry cleaners, a laundrette and fast-food outlets.

There was also the Gifu Prefecture Library which is separated from the Art Museum by an elegant brick road which, at night, is illuminated by 19th Century gas lamps. All this just a short bike ride from home past the inevitable rice fields which flank the Beltway at this point.

These facilities proved invaluable for me. I had the occasional naughty plateful of junk food at Mos Burger. I bought a couple of suits at the outfitters, Meisin, for about £30, shirts and socks at give-away prices, and a full-length, black leather coat which made me look like your friendly neighbourhoood Gestapo officer and which seriously bumped up the points on my loyalty card.

I bought incense and touch-operated table lamps at the fancy goods store, Bulldog, and plants at the DIY store, Mammoth. I discovered baked beans in the Valor supermarket (although I shopped mainly at Sanshin because it was a little nearer and much cheaper) and I got my hair cut at a unisex salon called 'Yours', whose owner had once spent a couple of weeks training at Vidal Sassoon's in London.

You could tell he'd been to London, I met him one evening in *yoro no taki* and he proudly came out with the extent of his knowledge of English. 'This is a filthy pub!' he grinned.

A slightly longer cycle-ride away was the 100-yen shop. Everything cost just 105 yen (VAT is a massive 5% in Japan!) which is about 60 pence, depending on the exchange rate.

Here I bought kitchen utensils, crockery, glasses, boxer shorts, coat hangers, electrical adaptors and extension leads, stationery, *origami* paper, etc. etc. This was a real Aladdin's cave and I think the best bargains were the CDs. I bought a few CDs of Beethoven and Mozart, as well as a pile of Japanese music, and I now have quite a collection of *very* traditional music and song, which, admittedly, is an acquired taste, but if you are into drums and wailing this is just the ticket.

Almost opposite the kindergarten, along a main road pleasantly lined with shady trees and flowering shrubs, was the convenience store, Mini Stop. This is where I paid my electricity bill and sometimes used the photocopier and fax machine. Convenience stores, *kombini*, abound, are open all day every day and seem mainly to sell snacks, booze and instant noodles.

I was once tempted to buy one such product purporting to be cheese curry, purely out of some sort of macabre fascination, but I bottled out in the end and bought a 'prawn' one instead. I expect it tasted the same as the cheese curry. Do prawns eventually turn cheese-flavoured? As well as Mini Stop there is Circle K, 7-11, Coco, Lawson Station etc. but my favourite was Sunkus, if only for its name. The Japanese pronounce it 'Sanks', but I always referred to it as 'Belgrano's'.

There wasn't a Belgrano's in Nishinoshō, but there was, a short walk away in Kashima-chō, a bicycle shop. A wonderful bicycle shop called Ogis which sold velocipedes of all descriptions.

My need was immediate because leaving the first flat meant leaving the bike as well, so I bought a bog-standard sit-up-and-beg Granny bike with a metal basket on the front and a carrier on the back. Just perfect for shopping.

It didn't have gears, but it had good brakes, a built-in lock on the rear wheel and a front light operated by a dynamo. Not everyone bothers with the lamp, and there was no back light because they just rely on the reflector. Brand new it cost about £45 and came with a year's guarantee. It would pay for itself within a few months by saving me bus and train fares within Gifu city. And I could get to the library more quickly. My happiness was complete.

*****

I joined the library, a vast, architecturally very appealing edifice built in the 1990s, which had hundreds of books in English, and a few in French and German, on the first floor. I took advantage of the Internet and the video library on the ground floor, where there was also a TV room with a huge screen, more a mini-cinema really, and a rather pricey restaurant.

There were study areas where I would wrestle with my Japanese textbooks, and a comfortable reading area where I could keep abreast of the British rugby results published in the English-language *Japan Times.*

The Sunday edition of the *Japan Times* printed articles from *The Observer.* There was also the London *Times* and, occasionally, the weekend edition of *Le Monde* which I would ostentatiously read to confuse the Japanese...they automatically assume that all *gaijin* are American.

In the hot weather I would read outside on sunloungers protected from the direct sun by a wide pergola from which hung long tails of wisteria, and alongside which flowed a little artificial stream only a couple of inches deep. Here toddlers, accompanied by doting grandparents, would paddle with fierce determination.

Alternatively I would sit in the little park in front of the Art Museum, a thoughtfully laid-out area with lawns that gently sloped down to an ornamental stream, a collection of aesthetically positioned modern sculptures and dozens of trees, each one labelled with its genus in both Japanese and Latin.

The scene was idyllic, all was calm and harmonious, I felt at one with the perfection and symmetry of my environment, my *wa*, my inner peace, knew no greater depths of tranquillity.

Then I would go home and apply a powerful medication to my mosquito bites.

****

CHAPTER 3

NIHONJIN

I have entitled this chapter *nihonjin* (Japanese people) because that is one of the most commonly over-used words in the Japanese language. It is more than a word, it is a concept, a statement of identity and belonging to be trumpeted loud and often, a quasi-religious, almost mystical, legalised narcotic upon which the Japanese are permanently stoned out of their minds.

It is a widely-held view by the Japanese that they are a world apart from other nations, that they have little or no desire to get too close to outsiders. Although they are welcoming and generous to the extreme in their dealings with *gaijin*, there is always the question hanging in the air: is the welcome extended out of a sense of duty, *giri*, or is it out of a sense of pity for the poor, sub-human and semi-educated barbarian?

Thus they consider their language, history, diet and culture to be too esoteric for any non-Japanese to even begin to understand, that they are cerebrally different from everyone else on planet Earth, and that they are naturally superior and unique. They seem to think that they had suddenly appeared on their group of islands with no reference at all to, or help at all from, the Asian mainland. Dammit! They're just like the Brits!

Well, maybe. My first intensive contact with Japanese people was in the year 2000, when I squandered part of the lump sum that I was graciously awarded after what seemed like a succession of lifetimes teaching in comprehensive schools, on a holiday in Japan. I stayed with the parents of my number four son's[1] first Japanese 'girlfriend', a nice little lady ten years older than sprog four, and, therefore, of a compatible mental age, who had, by a circuitous route, spent several holidays with us as a house guest. These holidays were reciprocated, ergo my *séjour.*

The Satō family were great. They lived in a neat house with a lovely Japanese garden (lots of big stones, a stone lantern, a stone bridge and carefully arranged 'pompom' trees) in Aichi prefecture to the south of Nagoya on the Chita peninsular. In other words this really *was* the sticks!

Mr Satō worked for Mitsubishi, miles away, and left home at 5am, returning at around 7pm. when dinner would appear as if conjured up out of thin air. Mrs S. worked from home sewing car seat covers on an alarmingly noisy sewing machine which could do a pretty passable imitation of a pneumatic drill.

Mr S. didn't work at weekends, so he spent that time pursuing his hobbies of gardening and

---

[1] Number four son has learnt Japanese. Because he is the product of a comprehensive school education his English is, naturally, mumbled and mutilated. Older brother asked why he was learning Japanese. "Obvious," said I, "He can't speak English!"

drinking large quantities of Kirin Ichiban Lager, a refreshing beverage with an ABV of a paltry 5.5%. After dinner he would retire to the *wa-shitsu*, the Japanese room, and hit the whisky.

The *wa-shitsu* was typical, a plain room with a *tatami* matting floor, a low, highly polished table with exquisitely carved legs, a picture of Mount Fuji, a wood-carving of the Seven Happy Gods, and sliding panels, one of which concealed the Satos' sleeping area. There was an alcove with a hanging scroll and, oh yes, a TV set roughly the size of a small car and a cabinet full of Scotch whisky bottles.

On the day of my arrival, a Sunday, after a long flight through eight time zones, I was offered an early lunch and the chance to snooze a bit, which I gratefully accepted.

After my rest I wandered into the garden where Mr S. was tidying up the pompom trees. Upon seeing me he immediately broke off work, rushed to the garage and emerged with a couple of bottles of Kirin Ichiban from the capacious fridge.

We perched on a couple of tiny fishing stools and toasted each other like old comrades. The bottles kept coming. In the evening we went out for dinner to a sushi restaurant. Mr S. ordered a beer, drank it, fell asleep, woke up and ordered another beer, downed that one and slept until it was time to leave. The rest of us just got on with the business of eating, Mrs S. casting the odd affectionate glance at her loudly snoring hubby. Mrs Satō's hobby was giggling a lot.

I loved these people, I had a great couple of weeks in Japan. I used my JR rail pass to its fullest effect (unlimited travel on all JR lines, including the *Kodama* and *Hikori* bullet trains). I met many helpful and friendly people, I visited Tōkyō, Ōsaka and Kyōto and I resolved to return. Five months later I did.

*****

There are two kinds of *nihonjin*: Japanese men and Japanese women. The distinction between the two is most finely drawn on the train. Japanese men while away the tedium of the journey by engaging in one of three activities; a. reading a book or the paper, b. changing seats and c. sleeping. A fourth may be added after the mandatory after-work visit to the *izakaya*, i.e. engaging in raucous conversation punctuated with raucous laughter.

Reading is the least exciting and least demanding of these activities, but changing seats sets a real challenge for the purposeful business-suited commuter who needs to manifest some sort of individuality before becoming an office clone for the rest of the day. Sleeping has a deeply Zen-like quality which allows the practitioner to become totally detached from the world until he arrives at his destination refreshed and spiritually renewed. By some mysterious process he never oversleeps his stop. In reality the poor sod is still completely knackered from the day before and is running on automatic pilot.

But however he may have spent his journey, the Japanese man alights from the train with an identical facial expression to that of all his fellow travellers, to whit: one of utter bewilderment and anxiety.

One of my places of work was located in a dismal, soulless concrete sprawl called Ichinomiya, about halfway between Nagoya and Gifu. It was largely a commuter city, so, when I caught my train, the 'New Rapid', at 9.35pm the Ichinomiya lemmings would disgorge. The doors slid open and a wall of alcohol fumes hit one like a fist. About half the passengers got off, which meant that the train was still heaving with bodies and smelling like a four-ale bar. Some of the blokes were even sleeping standing up! I nicknamed this train the 'Kirin Ichiban Special' and eventually stopped taking it, preferring to travel on the far-less-crowded local train where I could get a seat and ogle the ladies.

Japanese women are subdivided into two sections: older Japanese women and younger Japanese women. The older ones usually travel in small groups, are often clad in the traditonal kimono, and spend their journey in polite, smiling conversation punctuated by the occasional giggle, demurely hidden behind a hand. The younger ones are usually dressed in the standard young lady uniform, the colour scheme varies but the style is identical, very short skirt, impossibly high heels, revealing blouse and a jacket of simulated soft leather.

These delightful nymphs spend their journey reading and sending text messages on their mobiles, reading *manga* (comic books) applying makeup, shaking their long silky hair and practising their full-lipped sulky pouts. They rarely communicate verbally. This is understandable, get one to smile and you are looking directly into the mouth of 'Jaws'. The shark-tooth look is considered to be a mark of beauty. Japan is every dentist's nightmare or every dentist's paradise, depending on how you look at it.

*****

The Japanese passion for uniforms begins at kindergarten age (ok, the kids don't get a choice but the process of indoctrination starts here) and lasts pretty well up to the end of your life. Kindergarten kids wear sweet little smocks and 'jolly-hockey-sticks' type straw hats; elementary school pupils seem to be reasonably free to wear what their parents choose for them. Their principal badge of identity is a yellow hat or baseball cap, yellow in order that these mites may be spotted from afar by motorists.

This imbues a sense of invulnerability in the child, with the result that they feel perfectly free to amble across streets or dash out from blind corners at full tilt on their bicycles, inches from the wheels of mighty trucks.

Junior and senior high-school students wear the following: for boys the uniform is usually a black, brass-buttoned jacket with a round stand-up collar and a chafingly uncomfortable white cellulose lining. For girls it is a navy blue skirt and a navy blue jacket with a sailor's collar, white blouse and extraordinarily thick white socks which look like leg-warmers. Just great in summer!

The office clone in the business suit is not a figment of my imagination, all business dealings are conducted in a uniform, group-based manner which allows no room for individuality[2], and the suit is a uniform.

The uniform for men at weddings is a black or dark blue suit, a white shirt, a sober tie and a 'don't you dare smile in the wedding photos' look. The uniform for women is usually the kimono and they aren't allowed to smile either. The bride and groom, resplendent in their centuries-old traditional uniforms, look downright miserable, the more miserable they look, the higher the needle rises up the ecstacy-ometer.

Security guards are frequently very old and very tiny men magnificently attired in white and gold braided navy blue uniforms with epaulettes the size of chopping boards which make the Duke of Edinburgh's best sailor-suit look decidedly dowdy, and taxi drivers wear peaked caps, bow-ties and clean white gloves. All drivers of passenger vehicles wear peaked caps and clean white gloves.

---

[2]   If, as an up-and-coming Japanese business team player, you have a great idea, sit on it unless you want to be put in charge of ordering paper clips for the rest of your career. Similarly, as a big hitting baseball star, don't hit too many home runs or you'll be on the bench for a lengthy spell. Being Japanese is about doing it the *corporate way*.

Japanese train drivers are joy to watch. Their cabin is separated from the passengers by a glass panel, through which every movement can be observed. I now know why the trains are so invariably punctual. The driver constantly refers to a route/time plan which has a transparent, red-bordered slide that he (and sometimes she) adjusts as the train continues its journey. There is also a digital clock which counts down the minutes and seconds between stops, so that the driver may modify the speed of the train to ensure accurate timekeeping.

He (or she!) raises a white-gloved left forefinger and then points to every marker along the route that announces an approaching signal, level-crossing etc. When an apprentice driver is at the controls he is accompanied by a white-gloved instructor who leads the new boy in a two-handed, synchronised, clockwork hand-jive.

Building workers, road menders etc. usually wear incredibly voluminous trousers which are held tight around the ankle so that they may be tucked into curious split-toed rubber boots similar to the footwear worn by the feared assassins, the *ninja*. On their heads they wear a (usually) white towel as a protection from the sun, most of them sport a fierce straggly moustache and their proud, almost haughty, bearing reinforces the *ninja* look.

At all roadworks, however minor, the public are protected and guided by supervisors dressed in a smart blue battledress, a hardhat and high-visibility reflective webbing.

These cheery people guide traffic and pedestrians by raising a red or white flag or baton, they bow politely as you negotiate the hazard and they usually give you a huge grin and share few words to pass the time of day. These workers cannot be paid very much at all but they really seem to enjoy their work and their cheerfulness is infectious, at least it was for me.

I regularly encountered the same little chap at different locations as I rode around Gifu city and we seemed genuinely pleased to see each other each time he waved me past the hole in the ground.

The other chap who was pleased to see me now and again was the homeless guy who lived under a flight of steps leading to Nishi Gifu station. He kept the station area spotlessly clean and had a cheery wave for all the commuters who, naturally, ignored his existence. Well, he had long, unkempt hair, a straggly beard, what teeth he had left made his mouth look like a vandalised cemetery, and, horror of horrors, he didn't wear a suit.

One day I saw him searching for food in the rubbish cage in my block of flats. This froze my bones to the point of cycling immediately to the *kombini* in order to buy him a couple of rice-balls, *onigiri*, a cold bottle of green tea and some chocolate. As I cycled past him I placed the bag in the wheelbarrow he always pushed around. We said nothing; his eyes did all the talking.

*****

The above observations are but external views, the Japanese 'on the surface' as it were. In total contrast, however, I found genuine warmth and kindness in most people I met (sure, there were exceptions) and none more so than in hospital. In the autumn of 2001 I decided to contract a mystery illness, which led me to believe that I had caught a particularly virulent, and exclusively Asian, variety of influenza. I had never felt so miserable and so alone in all my life.

I managed to get to hospital and the consultant, who happened to be one of my star English language students, the Associate Professor of Medicine at Gifu University and a leading world authority on pulmonary disorders, took one look at me and diagnosed pneumonia. An X-ray and blood test confirmed his diagnosis and I was taxied off to the Gifu National Hospital, the *Gifu kokoritsu byōin*, on the eastern outskirts of the city.

My new doctor spoke a little English, mainly medical jargon, but no one else spoke a word and I think I was the first European to have ever occupied a bed in the entire history of the hospital. My colleague from work brought a few essentials from my flat miles away, and other colleagues showered me with gifts: chopsticks, five towels, a teacup, a coffee mug and a shopful of fruit. I was also visited by my eminent student and by 'Hankyhead', who brought me a lovely basket of flowers from the regulars in the coffee shop.

Amongst the few essentials that I had requested was my dictionary and the 'Handbook of Japanese

Verbs', one of a great series of Japanese-English language works of reference published by Kodansha. Armed with these two books I decided to use the hospital as my very own private university, I wasn't interested in television, I had time to kill, so I embarked upon the syllabus that I had written for myself in my head.

I chatted away to the nurses, blatantly wielding my verbs handbook,[3] I regaled people at mealtimes in the dining room, I teased the cleaning staff etc., and, joy of joys, I got positive and good-natured responses. Other patients, some terminally ill with lung cancer and wheeling around their personal cylinder of oxygen, shared mandarin oranges, pickled plums, yoghurt and so on with me. They would offer me green tea or Oolong tea. They would share cakes or crackers that their visiting relatives had brought and I would reciprocate as best, and as politely, as I could.

Above all, they <u>talked</u> to me and I really began learning the language. I think I learned more in ten days than I had ever thought possible and I will be eternally grateful to those sympathetic and very patient patients for all their help, understanding and friendship.

It was only two days before leaving hospital that I met Mr Mutō Shoichi, a very frail, elderly gentleman of eminent scholarship who spoke

---

[3] One phrase that I practiced on a, shall I say, not too skinny nurse was, '*kanojo wa takusan taberu noni, futorimasen*' which means, 'Although she eats a lot, she doesn't put on weight.'

excellent English and who shared the *Times* and the *National Geographic* with me. Delighted as I certainly was to make his acquaintance, I'm glad that I did at the end, rather than at the beginning, of my stay in hospital, for the obvious linguistic reasons. Oh how we hugged each other as I left the ward. My doctor gave me a parting word of advice:

'Change your brand to Super Lights.'

It isn't that difficult to make contact in a confined space like a hospital, a restaurant or a bar. The Japanese are very inquisitive people. There are three main questions that they need answers to: a. your nationality, b. your age, and c. your blood group. When they ask you your name you know that they have stopped being just curious and have now become interested. Indeed, at a later point during my stay, I was asked by a pal in a pub if I would perform his brother's wedding ceremony. Seriously! Anyone can officiate just as long as they have a licence, but I didn't, so there we are, although I knew a couple of Americans who made this into quite a lucrative sideline.

When I felt fit enough, on my return to normality, I popped across the road to *yoro no taki* to get reacquainted with my friends. The very first friend that I had made in the *izakaya* was Nōnaka-*san*, a repairer and small-time wholesaler of skis and snowboards. He spoke a little, rather halting,

English and I spoke a little more, but still rather halting, Japanese, so we were made for each other.

We shared similar interests, beer, food, *saké*, food etc. and I referred to him in correspondence home as 'Mr No Knackers.' I translated this for him and he didn't seem to mind. He proudly[4] introduced me to his friends Kiyōtaka-*san* and partner Kotoe-*chan*, the latter being a petite thirty-something who could drink extraordinary amounts of beer in very quick time and remain completely sober, if purringly friendly.

The four of us got together at fairly frequent intervals, we went to hot springs, we had house-parties at my flat, and we went skiing on the best slopes in Gifu Prefecture, a very popular area for skiing in Japan. The other three were expert skiers; in fact Kiyōtaka was a qualified instructor who, on one occasion, put Kotoe-*chan* through an official test. He failed her! After my first tentative descent I looked behind and thought I could see two *almost* parallel, and very wobbly, brown streaks of rust, not having been skiing for years.

These lovely people were not just amused to have me as a slightly eccentric toy, they were genuinely interested in bringing me into their culture whilst learning from mine. In fact Kiyōtaka asked me to teach his teenaged son French, which I attempted to do.

If you totally ignore geography, history, religion etc. you find that the everyday concerns of life, i.e.

[4] Proudly because I was his very own funny little *gaijin*!

41

eating, drinking, sleeping and procreating cross continents. The only difference that I can detect is that, in Japan, the latter is conducted in private. As stated earlier, 'Dammit! They're just like the Brits!' applies, with the minor exception that, unlike in my home town of Brighton, they don't shag on the beach.

So, what of Kotoe-*chan*? Oh, whatever... she never asked and the beach was miles away. Hey-ho!

But, as ever, you have to be wary. I knew a little guy in *yoro no taki*. He was aged about 45, stocky, crew-cut hair, hard looking, called Yama-*chan*. He never appeared to pay for his food and drink, had his own reserved table, a little group of sinister-looking chums, etc. He swore blind that he wasn't *yakuza*, mafia, but I wasn't convinced. Our customary greeting was a tactile exchange of clenched fists, knuckle to knuckle.

One night I was having a quiet bite to eat after work when a mutual lady acquaintance stormed into the pub, demanding to know what I was doing there. Japanese ladies can be so possessive, even on a casual basis. I think she was worried about my health. Anyway, it transpired that Yama-*chan* had phoned her on his mobile, just to mention I was there. Some pal! I asked him, later, if he was a policeman. He almost choked on his squid.

He had good reason to blanche at the word 'police'. A major criminal case was hot news during my time in Japan. I took a keen interest in this story, as my number four son was living in the same city at roughly the same time.

This saga involved the Wicked Woman of Wakayama, a middle aged, well off lady who, so the story goes, was heavily committed to dispensing largesse amongst the local population. She was a well-respected pillar of society who threw a garden party for about 100 people.

Parties in Japan are not stand up, circulate, socialize and dance-a-bit affairs, they are sit down and eat occasions. There is also plenty to drink, of course.

To this end the hostess had transformed her garden into a tented banqueting room where she treated her guests to lashings of curry and rice. What she did not reveal was that she had liberally laced this delicacy with a toxic substance which hospitalised over 60 unfortunates and killed three of them. Plod *san* started to smell a rat and the lady was eventually brought to trial.

The upshot was that she was found guilty of murder. The death penalty, by hanging, is still applied in Japan, and that is what she was sentenced to. Now, I am far too set in my ways to bother about political correctness, the next step is the Thought Police, so I have no problem with the concept of dispatching wicked citizens.

My only concern is this: there is no official executioner in Japan, so the concluding ceremony is performed by whichever prison officers happen to be on duty at the appointed time. This must be very traumatic for them and, although there are only about two hangings a year, the problem must be addressed one way or the other.

Another acquaintance, a bone-setter whose services I would later require,[5] to whom I was introduced by Mr No Knackers said, about me, 'I can't get my head round this. He looks European but sounds Japanese!' I was chuffed about that and went on to impress him even more by demonstrating my local knowledge and naming the Mayor of Gifu City. Was he surprised? Just a touch, and I let him dangle a bit until I coughed the truth.

One of my students was the Mayor's next-door-neighbour and they shared the same family name. I coughed up because people who are not always entirely honest are always found out sooner or later. So, all you lads and lassies in the Palace of Westminster: watch it! And that's the only moralising that you'll get in this book!

Yet one more cultural divide had been bridged. Yes, I suppose it had, but there then remained the question of arm-wrestling, which, apparently, is a way of getting to know people. This is where I met Kazumi. Kazumi was a member of the SDF, i.e. he was in the army.

Standing at five-foot nothing, and being a total mass of muscle with a shaven head welded directly on to his shoulders, he appeared to me to be the most user-unfriendly invention since the first 'hack it.... oh, dear, I've just lacerated a thumb' tin opener. There were two other Kazumis, taller,

---

[5] I fell off my bike. 'Nuff said!

more slender, but each looking as if a 'wee little murder' would give a slight kick to their otherwise lacklustre existences. So I was challenged to take them all on at arm-wrestling. Kazumi was first off the blocks. He pretty soon disposed of me, but he had the grace to concede that I was 'very strong', or was that just *giri*?

The other two slender mortals I saw off in a trice, if only because they were somewhat more tiddly than I was. Come on, admit it, would you arm-wrestle at all if you were totally in control of your faculties? This little victory, however, was enough to cement an eternal friendship which, through the medium of 'Heavy Metal', linked my wondrous western background to their perceived humdrum lives.

They were a Metal band. My firstborn son and heir is a bass player in a Metal band. They loved his band's demo CD and did their best to reproduce the sound (noise, din, cacophony?) belted out by this prophet from afar. Here, at last, was a meeting of cultures, a symbiosis of east and west, a melting pot of...oh, nonsense! Just lads being lads.

A pause for thought. These young men were the age of my children, as were the only *gaijin* with whom I socialised on a regular basis. These were two Australian workmates, splendid fellows called Cameron Phipps and Rohan Charlton, who were so wholly straightforward, dependable and genuine in their friendship, good nature and likeability that the question of age difference just never arose. The same applied to Kazumi and pals.

And these lads found a base, my little flat, where they could drift in and out whenever I was at home, and where they could unwind and listen to my lad's demo CD *ad nauseam*. If the Japanese television channels had had any imagination there could have been a whole thrusting, issue-based, Paxman hound-alike and flay-the-skin-off-this documentary starring me and my pals just being us, at peak viewing time. 'Why do you associate with this *gaijin*?' 'You go into his <u>home</u> and you haven't been inoculated?' 'Don't you just stare very rudely at him like the rest of us do?' 'How old is he?' 'Tell us his blood group.' 'What do you mean you don't know? Are you really Japanese?'

Alas, television was much, much more limp-wristed, as we shall see next.

****

CHAPTER 4

TEREBI

I didn't bother getting a TV set at first. I had watched a few hours of television whilst staying with the Sato family and when I was in hospital, and, apart from the *sumo*, there was very little that I didn't consider to be utterly dire.

There were endless talk shows of which I could understand precious little. There were bizarre eating contests which turned my stomach, in-depth focuses on local volunteer groups dedicated to slowing down traffic even more or preventing dog owners from allowing their mutts to mess the streets, how to get the best out of your microwave oven, etc. etc.

Shortly after coming out of hospital, however, a friend offered me a small TV set for nothing, and thus my viewing career was launched. Well, sort of.

Soon after I took possession of the TV I had the NHK man knocking on my door asking for licence money. How did he know that I had a telly? Did my pal grass on me like Yama *chan*? Was the homeless guy an undercover TV detector? Anyway, I paid some of it, only to find out later that this payment is purely voluntary. Next time he came I had forgotten every word of Japanese I had ever learnt. And the next.

Eventually he gave up and never came back. I felt a bit sorry because he was a nice man and it can't be an easy job dealing with awkward people like me.

Because I lived my life back-to-front I had all the early part of the day until about 2.45pm to explore the wonderful world of Japanese TV. I quickly got into a routine of timing my visits to the shops, library, launderette and ciggy machine to fit around my <u>must watch this</u> schedule.

Once the magazine programmes for housewives had ended, *mé-téré* (aka Nagoya Television) devoted its airtime to a succession of creaky TV series dating back a good twenty years. I soon got hooked on a ludicrous costume drama entitled '*Momo Taro – samurai*'.

Not far from Gifu city, on the Aichi bank of the Kiso river, lies the small city of Inuyama which is home to the one remaining privately owned castle in Japan. It is the location of the Meiji Mura - an open air museum of relocated significant buildings from the Meiji period (1868-1912), the Japan Monkey Park, Little World, and the Momo Taro shrine. Legend has it that the infant Momo Taro sprang fully formed from a giant peach (*momo* is Japanese for 'peach') and grew up to become a *samurai*.

In this creaky TV series Momo lives a quiet, gentle life in a castle town, chatting benignly with his simple townsfolk friends, drinking tea or, sometimes, *saké*, helping to build irrigation systems from lengths of bamboo, being really nice to children and so on. It's all very charming and heart-warming until things start to go awry.

This particular castle town is swarming with evil rich men who live in big houses behind high walls and heavily guarded gateways, keep a retinue of murderous henchmen and plot to amass as much money as possible by the blackest means possible. Anyone who stands in their way is mercilessly and gruesomely dispatched, usually at night, by masked henchmen.

Yes, you've guessed it, the stander-in-the-way is always one of Momo's harmless little pals. His or her slaughter causes much grief amongst the hitherto happy community, and effects an 'Incredible Hulk' like transformation in Momo's personality.

The character of Momo Taro is played by a tall, drop-dead handsome actor called Takahashi Hideki, who has the most acrobatic eyebrows on TV anywhere. They are a sort of hairy back slash/forward slash combination, which can be raised and lowered independently of each other or simultaneously, as required. They swoop, they dive, they knit together, they knit socks! They are wonderful and are put to best use when Momo goes Hulk.

Cut to posh house. It is night time; Big Baddie is gloating over piles of money bars with henchmen in attendance. Suddenly a little dagger with a tinkly bell at the end of the handle embeds itself in the post near Baddie's ear. All rush out to be confronted by a figure wearing a devil mask, a very fetching

Armani kimono and swords whose handles are laced in white silk. Off comes the mask. Gosh, it's Momo! Identically clad minions (uniforms again!) rush from the wings to protect their master.

Now, my understanding of Japanese was almost nil at this stage, so I cannot faithfully reproduce the ensuing dialogue, but it went something like this:

Momo: (basso profundo. lentissimo) *Itchy knee bongo mass stereo. Joking king goes an' shits on a new zoo queue.*

Baddie: (quizzically) *Koochie-koo?* (angrily) *Beano … double rubber band-oh. SMASH!*

Baddie's minions unsheathe their swords, but Momo swiftly, and <u>without shedding a single drop of blood</u>, slays about half of them and turns to Baddie for a little growly chat:

Momo: (lentissimo) *Green queen's toe. Cream marrow motto...FISH!*

He disposes of the rest of the minions and the henchmen and then, his eyebrows squirming and struggling to remain attached to his forehead, confronts Baddie:

Momo: *Happy shoe. Home grown gnome goes an' chops up a nutty panda....HITS!*

He bloodlessly turns Baddie into bacon slices, has a bit of a heavy breathe, then calms down and the next thing we see he's changed back into his M&S kimono, is wearing his ordinary everyday swords and is doing a bit of eyebrow stretching in the teashop. Peace and happiness return to the castle town...until the next episode. The story line is always the same, but the fashions are changed to give work to unemployed kimono designers.

There are many similar series. Another favourite was '*abarembo shōgun*' (roughneck *shōgun*) whose storyline was almost identical to Momo's, but the hero was the military overlord of all Japan who amused himself by sneaking, unnoticed, out of his castle and pretending to be just another well-respected *samurai* who loved children, who dispensed infinite wisdom and who mucked in with the ordinary folk, until one of them fell foul of a rich Baddie who.......well, you get the picture.

It was never clear where this chap lived, the opening credits had him galloping along a beach set against the massive backdrop of Mount Fuji, and at various times in the programme his residence would be portrayed as either Shirasagi Castle in Himeji, or Nijō Castle in Kyōto, or both. Well he <u>was</u> the boss, he could live wherever he chose, I suppose.

*****

Moving on to the 20th Century, another <u>must watch this</u> was a Tōkyō-based cop show entitled *hagure keiji* (maverick detectives). Why 'maverick' is a mystery to me, because all the characters seemed perfectly trustworthy and operated, as far as one can tell, within the rule of law. For goodness' sake, these fellows put money in the call boxes when they rang up HQ, this series having been filmed years before the advent of the mobile phone.

Anyway the main rôle was played by an actor called Fujita Makoto, who portrayed a detective by the name of Yasuda *san*. He had a wonderfully lugubrious expression, that sort of hangdog look worn by Humphrey Bogart, so I naturally nicknamed him 'Humph'.

Humph was a widower with two daughters, variously in their teens and twenties, the series having endured for several years. These daughters largely ignored his existence, being preoccupied with fashion magazines, pop music and anything else that avoids getting a life.

A combination of all these factors probably accounts for the hangdog look. I suppose he <u>was</u> a bit of a maverick in that he never wore a tie, which must have got up the nose of his immediate boss. He, being skinny and bespectacled, and who commanded respect solely by virtue of his ability to rant petulantly, put me in mind of an accounts clerk suffering from terminal constipation. He was pretty inept, how he achieved his elevated position is beyond me.

The big boss was a bulldog-shaped, neck less, agricultural-looking type with crinkly iron-grey hair and a massive face which radiated a combination of serenity and world-weary authority. He was the only male officer in uniform, the rest, being plain-clothed policemen, wore suits, with the exception of one detective who insisted on wearing that type of loud check jacket that I would outlaw upon pain of a lengthy spell in the pillory!

There was a token lady cop, a petite thing with the sweetest face on Earth and who sometimes wore uniform and who sometimes wore tailored suits that left you in no doubt as to her gender. Ok, she was gorgeous and I only watched the show to catch a glimpse of the delightful Ms Okamoto, who still appears on TV and is still quite lovely.

The story line was always the same; someone got murdered, Humph donned a pair of white gloves and turned up at the scene of the crime long after everyone else had poked around, Mr Constipation sent out the team of detectives to arrest the wrong suspect. Humph got gloomier and gloomier until, having done a bit of thoughtful chain-smoking, and having had a casual chat with a cheery street-cleaner or some such menial, solved the mystery.

Accounts clerk did a convincing impersonation of a stuffed frog, and big chief allowed himself a wry smile and heaved his shoulders in an endearing, world-weary manner.

Humph then took himself off to his favourite bar with whose kimono-clad, *geisha*-coiffured owner he maintained a platonic friendship, and smoked his way through a flask or two of *saké*.

Sometimes he took lady cop with him. She fancied him rotten, but it never amounted to anything as they both got far too drunk to remember why they'd come out in the first place. And, of course, there were the daughters to bear in mind.

Daughters: *tadaima!* (pause) *tadaima!*[1] *..nani?*[2]

In the year 2002 Ms Okamoto appeared on a series of TV ads. for Aviva personal computers, in partnership with a former boxer by the name of Gatsu Ishimatsu. It told a story over the length of one year and was cleverly done. He was a layabout, she was his wife who, along with their feisty daughter, was taking lessons in computer skills.

He was reluctantly persuaded to come along and got into training using dumbbells. After almost destroying a couple of keyboards he settled down in class, and his nearest and dearest, sitting a few rows behind, smiled affectionately at his bent back. He turned to his wife and daughter and bestowed a radiant smile upon them. He was reading a girlie mag.

Eventually he passed the exam and became a big shot in the company. I much preferred the layabout, former boxers look very uncomfortable wearing suits. Gold Blend this was not!

---

[1] "I'm back!"
[2] "Eh? What?"

This gradually unfolding story, involving a sharply observed imitation of almost real family life, went slightly against the normal run of ads.

Many of these involved large numbers of similarly clad, or uniformed, people, sometimes men but mainly women, wearing inane grins and moving in unison to emphasise the universal benefits of purchasing whatever it was they were promoting. It could be it a cosmetic product or the services of an agency which will send smartly uniformed and inanely grinning plumbers to unblock your loo for 8000 yen. And jolly reasonable it is too when you compare this with British prices!

A TV ad. that I particularly marvelled at was for a power drink called Repobiton D.[3] This involves two drop-dead handsome and heavily muscled young men doing macho things like scaling a sheer rock face or coaxing a heavy motorbike across a flimsy slatted wooden bridge.

Something goes wrong, certain death looms, bloke A has to heave and strain to rescue bloke B, they achieve their goal and celebrate by downing a bottle each of the aforementioned elixir. In unison (how else) they slam the bottles down, only to reveal that the bottles are still full and the twist-caps are still firmly in place. (Did you here the one about the Irishman and the never-ending pint of Guinness?).

---

[3] Japan is awash with power drinks. My favourite energy drink was Pocari Sweat, if only for the name. (I've never seen a pocari but I've drunk a lot of its sweat!)

The ads. are, of course, the most important programmes on TV because that's where the money comes from, and all scheduling revolves strictly around their allotted screening slots. News reports are frequently cut off in mid-sentence so that viewers may be made aware that a particular brand of cook-in curry block is really the only way towards a happy life, etc.

I was once watching an exciting college rugby match, in the dying moments of which Ōsaka was making a nail biting extra-time effort to win the game, when it was curtailed by the word "End" in English. I never did discover the final score, but I learned a lot of useful information about one of the many loan companies to which millions of Japanese are in thrall.

The chat shows were little more than thinly disguised promotions for resorts, restaurants, household appliances etc.

These morning and evening chat shows were such a chaotic jumble of on-screen clutter and rank amateurism as to be watchable principally for their naivety. A typical show would involve a panel of seven[4] minor personalities banging on about the respective merits of a selection of natural hot springs, *onsen,* the joys of harvesting edible seaweed in the pouring rain, or some such informative tosh.

---

[4] It was usually seven. Seven is a supposedly lucky number in Japan, hence the completely cancer-free cigarettes, Mild Seven and Seven Stars.

Each panellist would have a glass of something in front of them, green tea most likely, which remained untouched for the entire programme. Their contributions would be lavishly subtitled, thus obscuring one quarter of the screen, the top left section of the screen would contain a reaction-orientated inset of an audience member or panellist other than the one currently talking, and the occasional cameraman or scene shifter would make an unscheduled guest appearance.

On frequent occasions the message being conveyed[5] would be supplemented by someone holding up an attractive, multi-coloured and computer generated placard, roughly twice A3 size. This placard would invariably wobble and parts of it would be obscured by the holder's fingers.

I did once see, on the uncharacteristically watchable morning show *Hanamaru*, a computer screen being used to convey a variety of information, but the presenter was so enthusiastic about the whole affair that he gave this screen a friendly pat with his podgy paw and wiped it clean. As always in these shows, everyone saw the funny side. Amateurish as they are, these shows are jolly occasions which cheer you up, so good luck to them.

Number One prestigious chat show was screened around 1:15pm and was hosted by a skeletal, but formidable, lady called Tetsuko-something with a hairstyle resembling a squashed

---

[5]   Facts and figures, survey results, where to buy the best *ramen* etc.

beehive-cum-cycle helmet. She wore a layer or several of makeup that diminished the impression that she had arrived on this planet a mere week after the Creation, and had an interviewing technique that suggested that if this woman had had a cleavage, she could have cracked walnuts in it.

Elderly she certainly was, doddery she surely was not. She appeared, kimono-clad, her hair a miracle of the scaffolder's art, on weekly quiz shows, and wiped the floor with every other contestant in sight.

There was also 'Who Wants to be a Millionaire?' with the immortal catch-phrase, *'finaru ansa?' 'finaru ansa!'*

The news programmes were also full of clutter, especially when a foreign statesman was featured. In the run-up to the Iraq war we saw the same images of George Dubya repeated over and over again. His words would be swiftly voiced-over in Japanese whilst subtitles provided the same message. The right-hand portion of the screen would confirm that this, indeed, was the President of the United States, and that, yes, he was speaking from Washington, of all places.

The left-hand side of the screen would convey further relevant information. Certainly *kanji* is very beautiful, but I would much prefer to watch the news without people trying to tell me what to think. And I would have just loved to have heard more from Dubya, a snippet referring to

'Our frenz an' naybors in the Mid Least'

had me thirsting for much, much more of his mastery of the English language and his knowledge of geography.

*****

The 2002 Korea/Japan World Cup was the inspiration for the TV channels to whip the population into a frenzy of panic by showing endless footage of rampaging English soccer hooligans for weeks prior to the event. They then attempted to calm everybody down by proudly displaying the newly issued police submachine gun.

The World Cup promised to be as exciting off the pitch as on it. In the event the Brits. behaved impeccably and were welcomed into Japanese hearts and homes; well, think about it, a two or three week long trip to Japan is way beyond the pocket of your average yobbo.

Number One good guy was the England skipper, David Beckham, whose spiky cockscomb hairstyle was copied by thousands of Japanese fans, most noticeably by a wheelchair-bound Tokyo great-grandmother who sported a purple Beck-alike.

Having valiantly led the team to a flabby defeat by Brazil, Becks returned now and then to Japan, became an icon and began, shyly and endearingly, to amass Fuji-sized piles of money by lending his name to telly-ads. for mobile phones, cars, etc. etc. etc. Posh joined him in some of these ventures. Boy, can she pout! She could almost be Japanese!

A close runner-up to David Beckham in telly-ad. appearances was the German goal keeper, Oliver Kahn, and his beautiful, but nonetheless girl-next-doorish, wife, whose smile could light up an entire city. Sorry Ollie, you're a great guy, but one thing has been puzzling me. If a player lands the ball in your mouth, does it count as a goal or a save?

Whilst on the subject of football (*sakka* in Japanese) I noticed that the emblem of the national team is the crow. I found this puzzling. Tōkyō is plagued with crows, according to what I saw on TV. They are everywhere causing a mess and a racket and they are spookily intelligent. They drop snails and other crunchy creatures into the path of oncoming traffic in order to save themselves the bother of peeling them.

Their most spectacular party piece is constructing nests from discarded coat hangers. There are tens of thousands of them, so imagine the daily tonnage of droppings. No, please don't! Add a pigeon to the team logo and it completes the picture, if you really want to admit that you are crap!

I didn't watch much sport on TV, I did get mildly interested in baseball and became a sort-of follower of Hanshin Tigers, but let's be honest, it's only rounders with crash helmets. The crowds are led, not so much by cheer-leaders as by orchestral conductors who signal to the supporters what to chant and when to chant it.

I did like *sumō*, however, and forced myself to stay awake so that I could watch 'Sumō Digest' after midnight during the odd-numbered months. On one memorable occasion the great *yokazuna*[6], Musashimaru, a man of enormous girth and who makes the 5'11" George Dubya look like a Hobbit, lost to a much smaller opponent. (I'd wager that Musashimaru hasn't been able to see his willy without using a mirror for years). Interviewed after the bout, this mastodon of some thirty stones avowed that, 'From today I'm taking up horse racing!' i.e. become a jockey.

*****

A saving grace on Japanese TV is the Education Channel, which offers well documented, imaginatively produced and impeccably presented programmes on Japanese and World history which fully address the issues of Japanese behaviour and atrocities of the 20th.Century.

There were natural history programmes, traditional *nō* and *kabuki* theatre, traditional music played on the *koto, shamisen, shakohachi and taiko*,[7] and workshops in the techniques of *go.*

There were foreign-language learning programmes in American English, British English (well done BBC!), French, German, Italian, Spanish, Portuguese, Korean and Chinese. I tried Chinese for about five minutes. One o'clock in the morning

---

[6] Wrestler of the highest rank. There are three, not one of them Japanese (two Hawaiians and a Mongolian).

[7] Traditional musical instruments: 13 stringed harp, three-stringed 'banjo', bamboo flute, drum.

just isn't the right time. The American English programmes were a depressing confirmation that I understand but little of my native language, and they could easily have been presented by George Dubya:

Native speaker: *'Hey, Bob, what's up? How's the gabblesquawk going? Didya getcha ketchup fixed already?'*

I did actually work with a bloke who spoke like that. Nice guy, big smile, really friendly disposition, totally incomprehensible.

*****

Best of all I enjoyed the cookery programmes, mainly because they were short and readily understandable. There was this great cookery prog. called the 'Passionate Chef' which featured a chap who looked like a *samurai* minus his armour doing karate kicks in the opening credits and whose mission in life was to wheel some poor, dim, city-dwelling bimbo around the local supermarket, show her what <u>real</u> food looks like, i.e. it doesn't come in tins or cartons, invade her gruesome kitchen and produce a well-balanced gourmet meal which appeared to consist mainly of undergrowth.

A <u>must watch this</u> favourite was the 'really mouth-watering and entertainingly different mini-masterpieces for the whole family which you can knock up in a mere fifteen minutes plus preparation time' show (I'm paraphrasing here). This was hosted by a nice little roly-poly lady called Kaminuma Emiko and which featured, in turn, three eminent (male) chefs.

Number One was a tall, bespectacled, academic-looking type who put me in mind of the above-mentioned constipated accounts clerk and whose smile signalled a warning that he just might bite into your head.

Number Two was a small, slightly sumoid and very jolly rotundity who appeared to advocate keeping the ingredients as raw as possible prior to serving, and Number Three was a tiny chappy with twinkly eyes and a Zapata moustache which seemed never far from being flung into the pan along with the rest of the seasonings.

The programme was both educational and fun, a well-known personality would be roped in to learn how to peel, cut, slice, mix and cook whatever dish was being presented. These dishes were often European...I discovered at last that I had been making mayonnaise perfectly correctly for thirty years. What a relief!

The personality was *in situ* for a week, during the course of which he or she learnt how not to sever a finger and how not to wear more food than you cook. The final tasting was an accolade to the wisdom, expertise and imagination of the trio of culinary demigods.

The most degrading cookery show I saw was one which assembled a number of poor, dim, city-dwelling bimbos who were forced into producing twenty-minute masterpieces à la 'Ready, Steady,

Cook!' in front of a panel of eminent male chefs. The final results would be offered for consumption to the said culinary sages, who would grimace, gag and leave the studio, ostensibly to vomit, whilst the poor little bimbos would pleadingly assert that hubby really did appreciate their cooking.

A scoreboard was posted in the studio and the name of the relevant bimbo was affixed in order of merit. I saw one show where the one of the judges left, not only the studio but also the building, to affix the name of a particularly unfortunate hazard to digestion in the car park. Everyone laughed uproariously, none more so than bimbo herself, because that is how the Japanese deal with adversity. Not too many centuries ago she would have slit her throat in a ritual suicide, *seppuku*, before being beheaded to shorten the suffering.

Now <u>that</u> really would make great TV!

****

CHAPTER 5

RYOKŌ

It's springtime, late March, early April, you have a Thursday off and you really need to get away from the city. Follow the road westwards past Mount Ibuki, head slightly northwestwards and you find yourself in stunningly beautiful, mountainous countryside which subtly changes at every bend in the road.

Here a river tumbles over a steep, rocky bed, there a valley is given over to scattered dwellings, intensive cultivation and terraces of rice. Around the next bend half a mountain has been hacked away to provide the raw materials for the feeder roads to the new Nagoya Airport which is built on a man-made island in the Bay of Ise.

The road winds, climbs and falls, the traveller is alternatively blinded by the sun and shaded by ramrod-straight pines and cedars, bamboo groves wave their delicate fern-like tops and the road signs advise you to beware of monkeys. Then, suddenly, after one final bend, in the immediate distance, there they are! The snow-capped mountains of Fukui Prefecture, framed by lesser, greener hills at the foot of which nestles the village of Neo.

Neo, *neomura*, is the village where, some 1,500 years ago, the Emperor Keitai took refuge from persecution and planted a cherry tree, and is now a tourist trap full of eateries and souvenir shops.

The (very) late Emperor must have foreseen this modernisation, commercialisation and exploitation of his refuge, *keitai denwa* being Japanese for 'mobile phone'. Mercifully the place appears to close on Thursdays, but the adjoining Usuzumi park doesn't and it's here that you can still marvel at the gloriously gnarled and knotted cherry tree, now supported by many timber props but still producing swathes of pink blossom right on cue year after year.

The actual age of the tree varies between 1,500 years and 800 years, according to whose account you believe, but there is no disputing that this is a very old tree indeed and has, quite appropriately, been designated a National Treasure. Set against the mountains of the neighbouring prefecture it appears a mere upstart in the chronology of nature, but stick a man in front of it and it assumes a significance and a spirituality approaching deification, especially if the man is using his mobile!

The deification of nature is widespread in Japan. Most Japanese family names are direct references to the natural or agricultural world: *Ishida*-rock/rice field, *Yamakawa*-mountain river, *Mizutani*-water valley, *Kuwanō*-mulberry field, *Takida*-waterfall/rice field, *Sato*-village.

In many places you will spot a tree or a rock with a stout rope tied around it. This shows that this natural feature is a *kami*, a spirit.

In the Inland Sea, the *seto nai kai*, there are three rocky outcrops, one large, two small, joined together, and to the mainland, by a huge rope of unimaginable circumference. There are *kami* everywhere, in trees, in lakes and rivers, in rocks, in forests, in the weather- holy places abound almost as profusely as *ramen-ya.*

Not that the Japanese are particularly religious, worship in a temple being mainly a preserve of the elderly, but they are highly conscious of the spirituality of life and will often say a prayer at a shrine on the way to work or to the pub. It is not especially indicative of faith, more of respect.

Early in 2003 there was a problem with fly-tipping alongside the Gifu bypass, so the local council solved the problem by erecting small, wooden *torii* (symbolic *shintō* gateways) at regular intervals along the road, thus instantly making it holy ground which no Japanese would disrespect.

It can be argued, of course, that the electricity pylons which scale mountain ranges, the diggers which rip huge lumps out of mountainsides and the asphalt that conveys you past these eyesores are a form of desecration. They certainly are, but nature itself is as guilty as man in its insistence on inflicting earthquakes and typhoons on itself.   In May 2002 I was enjoying a car ride in the mountains of northern Gifu, on the way to Takayama, when I saw a most extraordinary sight.

On the steep, forested slopes, hundreds of pine trees appeared to have been snapped in two halfway up the trunk, leaving a palisade of jagged stakes to mourn over the fallen tops. My travelling companion, born and bred in the region and as quintessentially Japanese as a *haiku*, could find no rational explanation for this heart-rending phenomenon.

I mentioned this to a student of mine, a forester, a short time later. His explanation was as simple as it was terrifying: the accumulated weight of the snow, following a succession of heavy falls, had done for the trees.

*****

Somewhat saddened by the death of all these trees, but nonetheless encouraged by new horizons to enjoy, we continued to the town of Takayama which, during the Tokugawa shōgunate, was the administrative capital of the Hida region.

Takayama was also the subject of my first pun in the Japanese language. There is a department store called Takashima-*ya*, so my little joke ran like this: *takayama shi ni wa, takashima ya ga arimasu ka?* (Is there a Takashima in Takayama?) Simply sidesplitting isn't it? Well, the people I tried it on were very polite about it. *Giri* again, I suppose.

On the outskirts of Takayama there is a huge temple, brand-new looking but built in traditional style, upon whose façade is affixed an enormous Star of David. Not for the first time during my time in Japan I was nonplussed. I asked my companion if this was '*really, surely not, it can't be, can it?*' a synagogue. No, no! No synagogue was this; it was the HQ of a particular sect of the *shintō* religion. Confusion reigned: on town plans the location of a *shintō* shrine is always indicated by a red swastika!

Takayama, as mentioned above, was prominent as a regional capital during the Edo period and the most important building was the Governor's residence-cum-administrative HQ, the *jinya*, an extensive single-storey wooden palace which seems to meander amongst private courtyards, secluded gardens, military exercise areas and vast storehouses.

All the rooms, except the kitchen, have *tatami* flooring and can be extended or reduced in size by the expedient of sliding panels, many of which are of traditional wood-and-paper design.

Some rooms have a fire pit sunk into the floor, a kettle suspended over the brazier to supply the hot water for the inevitable green tea, *ocha*. The kitchen has a solid wooden floor and in the centre of the room is a tiled plinth upon which stands a cast-iron wood-burning range. The only other room which is not 'carpeted' with *tatami* mats is the torture chamber, which has a floor of pebbles, and which neatly displays the various ways in which people 'helping with inquiries' were suspended, beaten, stretched, crushed, mangled and ultimately crucified, impaled, burned alive or beheaded. Well, it gets the message across!

Dating also from the Edo period (circa 1600 - 1868) is the Takayama *matsuri*, or festival. Indeed, there are two festivals, the Spring Festival in April and the Autumn Festival in October. The festivals began as just simple village 'beanos' but, as the status and population of Takayama, the centre of distribution for the timber industry, grew apace, they took on an aspect of friendly rivalry between various sectors of the town. This involved more and more sponsorship from wealthy merchants, *saké* brewers etc. Was this the dawn of commercialisation?

Both festivals involve hundreds of men pulling eleven or twelve huge, wheeled and elaborately decorated floats through the narrow streets of the old town, across the numerous little rivers and along to the Sakurayama Hachiman Shrine.

These floats are decorated with complex carvings of gilded wood and resemble mobile shrines. Four of them feature marionettes which represent various gods or members of the nobility and which are operated from within the float by puppet-masters. These figures gesture, turn, spin and jump in a convincingly lifelike manner. One float requires eight puppet-masters to operate the three marionettes that it features. Each festival lasts for two days and takes place both during the daytime and after nightfall, when the floats are illuminated by hundreds of yellow lanterns.

After buying the mandatory souvenir, in this case a pair of varnished wooden chopsticks (made on the premises and cost about £1.50) and after sampling the various different types of *saké* in a succession of small breweries, I followed my companion back to the car. We set off for another slice of culture, the World Heritage site of Shirakawago. Before reading any further please watch the classic Kurosawa film, 'Seven Samurai'.

*****

Did you enjoy it? Good, isn't it? Right, so you remember that little peasant village way down in the valley? Well that's a very similar setting to that of Shirakawago, a preserved village, a living open-air museum of thatched wooden houses (*gassho*) farms and a water mill which date from pre-Edo times. There are one-, two- and even four-storey structures, all with steeply pitched roofs to cope with the winter snow. There was still snow on the mountain peaks in May, but the valley floor was nice and warm and the rice was growing apace in the *tanbo*.

The air was still and the near-silence contrasted sharply with the racket that you get in the city. I mentioned a water mill. Remember the mill in the film? There was this constant 'THUMP THUMP' emanating from it. This was the sound of a massive vertical beam being alternately raised and released to pound the grain into flour, rather than to grind it as in European mills.

Rather than being an intrusion into the near-silence, this rhythmic dull thudding seemed to complement it and serve as the only marker of the passage of time in a community that time, on the surface at least, seems to have overlooked.

History is ever-present in Japan. Two major routes, the *tōkaidō* (east sea road) and the *nakasendō* (inner mountain road) linked the old capital, Kyōto, with the centre of the Tokugawa fiefdom, Edo, which is now Tōkyō. Traces of both these ancient thoroughfares remain, and in the south east of Gifu prefecture, on the border of Nagano prefecture, lie the *yamaguchi mura,* the 'mountain pass villages' of Magome and Tsumago.

Here original houses, shops and tea-rooms, with their black-painted slatted sliding doors and grey-tiled roofs and first-floor canopies, hug the steep hillsides and afford views of the distant Southern Alps of Nagano *ken.* Traditional crafts, woodcarving, umbrella making, the preparation of sweetmeats (very sweet!) and the weaving of conical rice-straw hats, which are surprisingly waterproof, are on display at every turn.

I bought an umbrella in Tsumago, a traditional affair constructed of bamboo and oiled paper and which, also, is amazingly waterproof, much more so than the nylon disaster that I bought at the station one inclement day and which was completely useless in the rainy season.[1]

*****

Many of the towns and villages that I visited on my journeys, my *ryokō*, seemed to specialise in one traditional art or craft or another. On the shores of Japan's largest lake, Lake Biwa, lies the

---

[1] I didn't use the traditional umbrella, however, because it doesn't go with a business suit and, as a *gaijin*, I was visible enough anyway without looking a complete prat!

town of Nagahama where glass blowing is the local speciality.

Gifu city is renowned for exquisite paper lanterns. The nearby village of Seki is famous for cutlery, which really means knives, and there still remains a forge where the weapons of the *samurai*, the long sword, *katana*, and the shorter *wakizashi*, are still painstakingly produced in a laborious process which involves folding and hammering each length of steel thousands of times in order to achieve a deadly, yet strikingly beautiful, razor-sharp blade.

Meiho is famous for its delicious, slightly spicy, ham.

In neighbouring Aichi prefecture the towns of Seto, east of Nagoya, and Tokoname on the Chita peninsular, are pottery towns. Pottery is central to a traditional Japanese meal, western style matching dinner services being considered unimaginative, if not vulgar. The different shapes, designs and hues offered at a Japanese table are an integral part of the eating experience and help to enhance the textures and colours of the 'food sculptures' that are aesthetically presented to the appreciative diners.

Further afield the city of Kyōto specialises in folding fans, and Kōbe is a major producer of saké.

Gujo-Hachiman, in the heart of Gifu *ken*, is noted for the pure quality of its water which permeates the surrounding mountains and criss-crosses the town in numerous streams and which trickles out of many drinking fountains. If the drinking water in my flat was like satin, this was pure silk.

Of equal note: each year the Hachiman *odori* is performed by what appears to be the entire population. The *odori* is a folk dance which continues with relentless repetition throughout the night and which, in part, imitates the actions of sailors looking for landfall. This is particularly curious as Gujo-Hachiman is about as far from the sea as it is possible to get on Honshu Island.

The town is dominated from high above by a wooden *daimyō* castle (restored in 1933) part of whose inner defensive wall is a substantial tree, and which has very creaky floors and staircases to alert the occupants to the unwelcome nocturnal presence of any would-be thieves or assassins. Personally I think that most potential intruders, however fit, would be just too knackered to pose any sort of threat after shinning up the considerably lofty perch upon which this castle sits. Merely driving up the winding road that now leads to it was exhausting!

*****

Any trip is incomplete without visiting an *onsen*, a volcanic spa where, after soaping, shampooing and showering off,[2] you can relax naked in the natural hot water that springs from the earth with

---

[2]   You must sit on a small plastic stool to perform your toilette, standing is decidedly infra dig.

beneficial effect. Itadori *onsen*, Shiratori *onsen*, Gero *onsen*, these are famed throughout Japan and attract large numbers of visitors, particularly Gero which boasts many large hotels and countless bathhouses.

There is a walled-off enclosure by the river where open-air nude bathing is enjoyed actively by the men in the water and passively by the residents of the overlooking hotels. Hot baths are a major part of Japanese life. Every *ryokan* has its communal baths, one for males, one for females, and every home, however minimal like mine, has a deep bathtub in which the effects of a long working day and a crowded, smelly train journey can be sloughed off. On the way back to Gifu city after one of our skiing trips my companions and I stopped off for an hour's hot soak and a comforting bowl of *tonjiru*, *miso* soup with pieces of pork, washed down with a bottle of Asahi Super Dry beer.

*****

Then I was taken to a foreign land! Beyond the mountains of Fukui *ken,* which I mentioned above, lies the *nihonkai*, the Sea of Japan, which sometimes laps, but more frequently buffets, the shores of Japan, Korea, China and Russia, and which nurtures its own people, lifestyle, landscape and weather. Here the soil is almost orange in colour, the people look different, they are noticeably shorter than the city dwellers of Gifu, weather-beaten and bright-eyed, and the villages hug the sea as if they were a part of it.

They are! This is a maritime community, a people inextricably linked to the capricious provider of their living, where the rice fields are separated from the beach by only a flimsy concrete wall and where the steep, almost sheer, slopes of the mountains leave only a narrow corridor where human habitation is possible.

Instead of seagulls, buzzards wheel and plane over the high tops and perch on lampposts and buildings, even in the city of Tsuruga. Even the traffic lights are different! In most of Japan the traffic-lights are mounted in a horizontal position, but on the *nihonkai* they are vertical in order to minimize the effects of the vast amounts of snow that that rage in from the Asian mainland every winter.

This is the coastline to which, in the 11th. Century AD, came the young Shikibu Murasaki, the teenaged daughter of an official of the the Imperial Court in Heian Kyō, the present-day Kyōto, whose father had been allocated an ambassadorial role in Echizen and whose duties included receiving eminent visitors from China.

Lady Murasaki's journey to Echizen had been horrendous, involving, as it did, a turbulent voyage the length of Lake Biwa and then a painful trek across the mountain barrier to the Sea of Japan. She missed Kyōto almost to the point of heartbreak, but she was a dutiful daughter and helped her beloved father in his tasks.

In the course of these duties she met a young, sensitive and highly cultured Chinese poet and formed a close, literary (if nothing else) relationship with him. They corresponded daily in esoteric verse, thus honing an extraordinary poetical skill in Murasaki which, after her eventual return to the capital, led her to write the *genji monogotari*, the 'Tales of Genji'.This epic story of love, passion and betrayal at the court of the Emperor is arguably the most famous work of Japanese literature, penned by a lady who cornered the market 800 years or so before Austen, the Brontes, Eliot et al.

So it was that I, almost 1000 years later, also came to Echizen and gazed across the same body of water that had brought, and had abruptly taken away, her Chinese inspiration. Were these brown, weather-beaten and bright, inquisitive faces the same that had greeted her? I wondered. By which precarious means had she got from one side of the village to the other? That road tunnel didn't look all *that* old! Was that mountainous backdrop (minus the power lines!) as she would have seen it? Did she feast on crab as I did, and was it local or was it brought from Hokkaidō, as was mine, in the summer months?

Today Echizen is almost obscured by billboards advertising crab restaurants. We probably did share the same epicurean experience, albeit one millennium apart, as I, clad in a *yukata*, a light summer kimono, and seated on a cushion at a low table in a dining room overlooking the Sea of Japan, was presented with a feast of assorted raw fish so fresh that it might have been taken from that same sea only minutes earlier. Sour pickles, tangy seaweed, steaming rice and warm *saké* combined with the setting sun and the bobbing lights of fishing boats to make this meal one of the most memorable that I have ever had.

*****

There remained one more goal to achieve, one more journey to embark upon, before I could even contemplate leaving Japan. I had to see Mount Fuji. In the year 2000 I had travelled four times by the bullet train, the *shinkansen*, past Fuji-*san* but had not once been able to see it because of unfavourable weather conditions, i.e. brilliant sunshine on the Pacific coast but a Fuji-obscuring mist inland. This, I since learned, is not uncommon, and it merely served to stiffen my resolve to gaze at this revered volcano, at present dormant but you never know.

The car-ride took about five hours because there is no direct route through the Southern Alps, you have to skirt them by heading north to Lake Suwa and then south-eastish to Yamanashi *ken* and Fuji Five Lakes, the most beautiful vantage point from which to enjoy the view.

This was great because Lake Suwa is the burial place of one of my favourite warlords, Takeda Shingen, who was a real thorn in Ōda Nobunaga's flesh. Please refer to the Kurosawa film 'Kagemusha' for further details. So, after making a respectful bow towards the lake whilst martially intoning Shingen's catchphrase *ugokuna!* (Don't move!) we continued the journey to Yamanashi.

On the way I saw another remarkable sight, a flock of sheep! Obviously kept for novelty value, lamb just isn't on the menu in Japan.

We made our long, gradual descent to the city of Kofu and it was from there, through the haze, that I had my first glimpse of Mount Fuji. It was still some thirty kilometres distant but looked massive, its 3776 meters dwarfing the mountains that surround Kofu. Shrouds of mist alternately covered and revealed its flat, snow-covered summit and its flanks, today, were of a greyish blue shade that subtly blended against a sky of a similar hue.

Finally, after nearly three years, there was my goal, and it had been well worth the wait. This time it was my lucky day, apparently the mountain had not been at all visible for the preceding month. The *kami* was on my side!

We crossed that last barrier of mountains and arrived in the heaven-on-earth that is the region of *fuji-go-ko*, Fuji Five Lakes, where Fuji-san seems to be the centre of the universe. It is glimpsed through the trees, it is reflected in the lakes, it appears to control the weather, sometimes hiding its flanks, sometimes hiding its summit, sometimes revealing its full, terrifying majesty as the whim takes it. Surely I was in the presence of a god, and felt more so when, later on, I was immersed in hot bath in a *ryokan* overlooking Lake Shoji with Fuji's great symmetry framed in the picture window.

The combination of mountain, lake and forest has always appealed to me, largely for the photographic opportunities that they afford than for some hankering after a simple life away from the modern world; I like my creature comforts too much.

We visited each lake in turn, Motosu *ko*, whose main attraction after the scenery, appeared to be a pleasure craft whose prow was graced by a large plastic swan's head. Shoji *ko*, the smallest lake, was reserved for rowing clubs, swimming being prohibited. Sai *ko* didn't seem to want too many visitors, the sparsity of parking places made that quite clear, but Kawaguchi *ko*, the largest lake, had a number of little beaches from where people can fish or hire rowing boats or paddleboats.

We chose to hire a rowing boat, as the paddleboats all had rather tacky swan's heads, and we spent a pleasant hour admiring the great mountain and riding the wash of successive squadrons of speedboats. Shoji *ko*, Sai *ko* and Kawaguchi *ko* are all really the same body of water, connected by an underground river (Kawaguchi means 'river mouth'). The fifth lake, Yamanaka *ko*, is some eighteen kilometres away, is closer to Fuji-*san* than the others, and boasts a mighty flotilla of swan-headed pleasure craft of every conceivable size.

Yamanashi *ken* is a wine producing area, the grapes are grown on vines which hang from pergolas, and so, naturally, we bought a few bottles to sample. The Japanese are great at copying technology and even whisky, but their wine leaves a lot to be desired. Imagine a blackcurrant cordial flavoured with barbecue lighting fluid and you get the picture.

The grapes are fat, juicy and delicious and are best left just as they are, to be eaten rather than turned into an accompaniment for boiled cabbage. Well, you can't have everything.

*****

It is significant, however, that in all of the places mentioned so far, I seemed to be the only *gaijin* to be seen. I wasn't particularly looking out for fellow Westerners, it wasn't necessary. Having spent all of my time in an almost exclusively Japanese society, I was accustomed to Asiatic features, speech patterns, dress, body movement etc.

Therefore, when I reached a major centre for international tourism, such as Kyōto, it came as a shock to see so many non-Japanese. They were backpackers for the most part, whose most distinctive characteristics appeared to be noses and legs of such length as to put me in mind of large, myopic wading birds. 'Myopic' because their facial expression suggested that they had no idea of where they were or why.

There were hordes (flocks?) of them and they were so fascinating that I could not help but stare in amazement. They craned their necks, they bobbed their heads, and they lifted their enormous feet in a slow undulation towards the next sight to gawp at. In a curious way I felt that my space had been invaded.

Marcus Grant

I had become Japanese!

****

CHAPTER 6

KYŌTO, NARA, HIMEJI

It is possible to get shrine-fatigue in Kyōto. There are more than 1600 Buddhist temples and 270 Shintō shrines in this, the seventh largest city in Japan with a population of 1.4 million, but which seems larger because of the expanses of city centre parkland which surround the former Imperial Palace, Nijō Castle and the Heian Jingu shrine. On the tourist map these places appear to be within walking distance of each other, located as they are close to the same major east-west thoroughfare, Marutamachi Street.

Do not be misled, as I was on my first visit to Kyōto, by the scale of this map. It is hopelessly inaccurate and must not, under any circumstances, be taken seriously. Unless, that is, you really enjoy walking for miles under a baking September sun whilst trying to keep to the tight itinerary of 'things that you really must see on your day trip to Kyōto' that you had written weeks before you even came to Japan.

By far the best way to get around is by the excellent bus service that costs a mere 500 yen for an all-day ticket valid on any route within the city. Outside rush hours the traffic flows surprisingly smoothly, so on my next visit, this time for two days, I took the bus.

The first stop was the Temple of the Golden Pavilion, *kinkakuji*, a faithful replica of a 15th. century temple which survived the upheavals of the *sengokujidai*[1], the Tokugawa regime, the Satsuma rebellion and World War Two, only to be burnt down by a mad novice monk in his twenties in 1950. Rebuilt in 1956 its classic proportions and gilded exterior transport you back to the time when, in Heian Kyō (Kyōto) at least, the marriage of Imperial, priestly and *samurai* cultures was reflected in the architecture as well as in the local cuisine.

This three-storey building, whose second and third floors are covered in gold leaf and are surmounted by elegant upward-curving eaves, is approached by a winding, tree-lined pathway, at the end of which the pavilion is revealed. Its imposing splendour is mirrored in a small lake where large rocks and judiciously planted firs lead the eye towards the temple and its backdrop of densely forested slopes. I had the impression that, in terms of both time and distance, I was about as far away from the modern era as it is possible to get.

Lunch consisted of a large bowl of *tempura udon* and a bottle of *Asahi* before setting off for the relatively nearby Ryōanji Temple. On the map, of course, it looks very close, but allow yourself about 25 minutes if you feel like a walk, or spend about the same time waiting for a bus if you are unlucky enough to have just missed one. The temple itself is a quietly understated black and white wooden structure at the top of a wide flight of stone steps.

[1]   The age of continuous civil wars

Remove your shoes, step on to the highly polished pine floor, turn left into the covered walkway and you are looking at a zen garden designed and laid down in 1473 by the gardener Soami. It contains no plants, just raked sand and fifteen carefully placed rocks, and has been the focal point for meditation for more than five hundred years.

The whirring and clicking of the tourists' cameras make meditation a little difficult today, but the garden remains a timeless enigma. Ryōanji also boasts a small circular well embellished with four *kanji* which, when combined with the central square character, spell the message, 'I know just enough'.

The visit to Ryōanji ends with a walk through its extensive and delightful garden, alongside a small lake near the shores of which is the meeting and eating house of the Kyōto Fried Tōfu Society, *agedofu* being a culinary speciality of the city and its environs. The tiny, delicate leaves of the many Japanese maples were just on the turn, promising a fiery November display.

This had been my second visit to the Ryōanji Temple, but, for my Japanese companion, Junko, it was the first, and she appeared to be delighted that I had found the well that I had been banging on about since leaving *kinkakuji*, having missed it the first time.

From Ryōanji, in north-western Kyōto, it seemed a good idea to visit the suburb of Arashiyama on the western edge of the city. This is a traditional area full of genuinely old houses, a river where boating is popular, and craft shops offering folding fans and hand-coloured fabrics. I bought a delicately scented, slightly pungent, folding fan and had my photo taken seated next to a *maiko-san*, an apprentice *geisha*, with a face painted pure white.

There are the inevitable rickshaw boys who throng every major tourist centre. We had a rickshaw ride which cost about £5 per minute but which, nevertheless, was enjoyable and, if you speak the local dialect, highly instructive[2]. More importantly, Arashiyama appears, so far, to have hidden its appeal from the flocks of wading birds that bob and squawk elsewhere in Kyōto.

We ate in a traditional restaurant in the Gion district that evening. Gion is famed for its *geisha* houses. Japanese restaurants, even modern ones like those on the eleventh floor of Takashima-ya in Gifu, have a raised dining area, carpeted with *tatami* mats bearing low tables at which you sit on cushions called *zabuton*, as well as conventional western-style tables and chairs at 'ground level'. I've always found sitting on the floor to eat rather challenging, as I need to have support for my back, and my knees seize up after sitting cross-legged for even a short time, so my heart sank a little when we entered the restaurant.

It had just a traditional raised eating area, but, joy of joys, there was a sort of pit under the table for your legs and, as it's almost a requirement to put your forearms on the table, I could enjoy my

---

[2]   I just contented myself with admiring the scenery!

meal in total comfort. And what a meal it was! Fresh raw tuna, deep-fried *tōfu*, quick-fried slices of tender, rare beef, rice, assorted vegetables, buckwheat noodles, *soba*, and a flask or two of *saké* followed by green tea and sticky, very sweet confectionary.

*****

Next day we took the bus to the Temple of the Silver Pavilion, *ginkakuji*, on the eastern side. Unlike the Golden Pavilion, there is not an ounce of precious metal to be seen, the *shōgun* who commissioned it in 1489 having died before the final touches could be applied and his successor taking the view that the money could be better spent (probably on himself!). It is, nonetheless, an exquisite little building which lies in a charming garden at the foot of a densely wooded mountain, similar to the setting of *kinkakuji* but affording wider views and a walking trail which brings one closer to nature.

Here I bought a *juzu*, Buddhist prayer beads which I have worn on my wrist ever since, and an imitation (i.e. blunt) *wakizashi* which, being the shorter of the two swords worn by the *samurai* class, I could practise drawing and sheathing in my flat without knocking things on to the floor and without removing my left thumb.

I resisted the temptation to stick it in my belt, next to my fan, much to Junko's relief; she had already made a comment about my white sweatband!

Marcus Grant

Well it might have been mid-October, but the temperature was still in the high twenties. We also resisted the entreaties of the rickshaw boys.

Our next port of call was the *heian jingu*, an enormous vermilion painted shrine modelled on the ancient Imperial Palace and being roughly one-third its size. It has a number of different halls, each with the traditional upward-sweeping eaves and emerald green rooftiles. After our tour around the quiet garden with its many water-features and colourful *koi* carp, we were lucky enough to witness the photo session following a wedding which had just taken place at the shrine.

As usual nobody smiled, but the wedding costumes looked just great set against this wonderful building. Then we went to hunt the wading birds.

We found them at Nijō Castle which, being in the centre of Kyōto, is well within loping distance of the station. Nijō *jō* was built for Tokugawa Ieyasu upon his accession to the shōgunate and where he spent some time before moving the capital to Edo. The crafty old racoon[3] wasn't taking any chances whilst living here, so far from his power-base in the east.

Every floor in this magnificently decorated, one storey palace squeaks at every tread. The flooring system ensures that each board moves slightly at the ends and a system of nails and hooks produces

---

[3]   In Japan the fox is considered to be rather a snobbish animal, cunning is attributed to the racoon.

a bird-like 'cheep', hence the name 'nightingale floor'. Try as you might, it is impossible to progress more than a metre without sounding as if you need oiling. The audience room has a dais next to which are sliding panels to hide the ever-alert bodyguards from view and the whole complex is surrounded by massive walls.

There is a representation of the audience room in the book 'Golden Screen Paintings of Japan' by Elise Grilli, published by Elek Books, date of publishing not given, but the painting dates from 1626. The overall impression of Nijō *jō* is one of aestheticism rather than of military functionality.

The interior walls were painted by the most famous and talented contemporary painters of the natural and animal worlds. The intricately-carved roof-support beams in the internal walkways drip with gold leaf and the *shōji*, when slid open, would reveal a rock- or water-feature, an interestingly-shaped tree or some other such tribute to the beauty of nature.

This palace-fortress was a magnet for the backpackers, understandably enough, but not everyone was impressed or happy. I overheard one gentleman from North America complaining bitterly, and at great volume and length, that the Nijō staff were incapable of speaking English.

This is strange, I was once a part-time multi-lingual guide in a famous building in the UK and I couldn't utter a word of Japanese, karate terms aside. (I was once asked by a lady visitor, from North America, if we had a bathroom. 'Certainly, madam,' I replied, 'we have a bathroom, should you care to take a bath. We also have a toilet, should you care to urinate.' Remarkably I kept my job!).

We took the subway to Higashiyama and thence proceeded by bus to Kiyomizu Temple. The Kyōto underground is suicide-proof; glass panels separate the platform from the track and sliding doors, precisely aligned with the carriage doors, open when the train arrives.

Kiyomizu *dera* is perched on a hill overlooking the city and has a vermilion-painted three storey pagoda, a vast wooden terrace which affords stunning views and three spouts of spring water, each of which visitors attempt to drink in turn. This complicated procedure is performed from a platform set behind the spouts, by using wooden ladles about six feet in length.

There are heavy iron contraptions which the warrior monks[4] of yore used to build up their strength, golden statues of the Buddha and a second, less garish, pagoda set peacefully in the lush woodland facing the terrace across a small valley.

It is best to make a visit in April, in order to enjoy the cherry blossom, or in November to marvel at the brilliant deep autumn reds of the maple leaves. The street that leads up to the temple is called 'Teapot Lane' because of the many ceramics shops which line both sides, Kyōto being also a centre of the pottery industry.

---

[4] Today, I observed, the monks still have contraptions into which, after devotions, they leap and drive home.

There is a very pleasant walk from Kiyomizu to Heian Jingu, which takes you through the Gion district past the Yasaka pagoda and the Yasaka shrine, a favourite venue for midnight prayers at the turn of the New Year. Huge crowds press into the available space and, as part of the ritual involves throwing a coin into a box with a slatted top, the worshippers at the front of the crowd are inadvertantly pelted with a shower of coins thrown by the mighty throng further back.

The shrine is approached from the eastern side through a huge vermilion *torii* which leads from a charming park, Maruyama *koen,* with its koi carp-filled ponds, its waterfalls, willows and little teahouses. As you head northwards towards Heian Jingu you pass more temples, including one of the largest in Japan, the enormous Shōren-in temple, built of massive timbers in whose assemblage not one nail was used. All ancient buildings just slotted together like some giant, three-dimensional jigsaw puzzle.

I have still to see the Sanjusangendo Temple which displays 1001 gilded statues of the Goddess of Mercy, the Fushimi Inari Taisha shrine which has over 10,000 red-painted *torii* stretching along a four kilometre path, the Gion Festival, when portable shrines, *mikoshi*, are paraded and the Jidai Festival, when citizens parade dressed in the costumes of the Imperial Court as would have been worn by the Lady Murasaki. These will have to wait until my next visit, it requires far more than just a few days to see everything that is worth seeing in Kyōto.

*****

About a half-hour's train journey away, south of Kyōto, is the even more ancient capital of Nara. More temples and shrines, of course, in slightly lesser profusion than in Kyōto but of no less importance to the religious and cultural history of Japan.

For me the focal-point just had to be the great temple of *tōdaiji*, another National Treasure, reputedly the largest wooden hall[5] in the world and which houses the *daibutsu*, a huge, bronze statue of the Buddha. The dimensions of this statue are awesome: it is 15m.(almost 50 feet) high, the head is 5.41m long and the ears are 2.54m long.

The detail is extraordinary, each fold in the garments, each tight curl of the hair, each line in the palms and fingers of the hand, and each petal of the 3.05m.high lotus standing next to the cross-legged Buddha is finely drawn in hammered bronze.

This breathtakingly colossal statue dates from the eighth century AD. It is guarded by great, fierce-looking warrior-gods and accompanied by the wife of Buddha cast in gold and seated nearby, her left hand raised in blessing in a mirror image of the raised right hand of the Buddha himself. An octagonal stone lantern, 4.62m. (15ft.) high and which also dates from the eighth century, towers

---

[5]   *tōdaiji* is a mere 1m.26cm. shorter than the 50m. high Arc de Triomphe in Paris.

above the mortals on their approach to the great hall..

The *tōdaiji* complex is situated, as are other religious sites, in the large and finely wooded Nara Park where over 1000 small deer roam freely among the visitors. Special biscuits are on sale for people to feed these delightful creatures, some of which bow respectfully before accepting the titbit. They are, of course, very popular with children and are, unlike me, totally at ease with them. How they manage to tolerate them is a mystery.

Japanese children never walk anywhere, they run! They run in parks, they run in streets, they run in supermarkets and in libraries, they run in shrine complexes and they invariably run into my viewfinder when I'm just in the process of releasing the shutter mechanism. They turn what are potentially marketable works of photographic art, not to say genius, into mere holiday snaps.

Some of these brats are just too blurred to make identification possible; I can't even track them down to wreak my revenge. What a shame! That torture chamber in Takayama looked so interesting and imaginative, so varied, so efficient!

At the eastern end of Nara Park is the Kasuga Taisha shrine, another product of the eighth century, and which, in effect, is four shrines in one. The chief characteristic of Kasuga shrine is the collection of more than 3000 standing stone and bronze lanterns, which line the ascending pathways, whilst hanging lanterns adorn the main shrine. These lanterns have been donated over countless years, the main shrine displays gifts of large barrels of *saké*, and the buildings are all pulled down and replaced every 20 years or so, but are carefully rebuilt in the original style that dates from the year 768.

The whole shrine area is situated on a wooded hill and the sunlight is filtered through the broad leaves of the trees, giving a mottled effect to the vermilion pavilions and the pathways. A trumpet is sounded in the evening to call the deer, which are considered to be divine messengers, to their pens. It is a very tranquil place.

As well as being the home of the world's largest wooden building, it is also the home of the world's oldest wooden structure, the five-storey pagoda at the Horyuji Temple. This extensive temple was founded in 607 by Prince Shotoku, the regent of the Empress Suiko, an ardent promulgator of Buddhism.

It is a complex of some forty-five buildings dating from the seventh to the seventeenth centuries and this, too, has been designated a World Heritage site. There are great statues of fierce gods, gardens, pompom trees and just about everything else that you expect to find in a Buddhist temple, including monks selling entry tickets and other monks sweeping the pathways with besoms.

As at *tōdaiji* there was, as far as I could see, no literature available in English, which really would have sent the above-mentioned North American chap into fits of apoplexy.

Back near the centre of Nara I decided that I needed some cash, so I had to find a branch of my bank. There was a thickset, besuited and bespectacled gentleman handing out leaflets for some *pachinko*[6] parlour or other, so I asked him for directions. This was one occasion when the Japan Tourist Office's endless depictions of the smiling, welcoming public face of Japan were completely at odds with reality. This guy repeated my exact words in a whining falsetto and a 'comic' accent, and then claimed not to know where the bank was. Junko was astounded that someone could be so rude.

My spoken Japanese was pretty good by this stage, so I thought that he was just poking fun at my Gifu accent. Nara is in the Kansai region where, instead of saying *'arigatō'* for 'thank you' they say *'okini'*, and other such differences. 'No', insisted Junko, 'He wasn't polite. He pretended not to understand you.'

No matter, we found my bank and I got my cash. On the way back we passed Mr Leaflet. I smiled evilly and said, *'ano, kono shigoto wa, tanoshii desu ka?'* (Do you enjoy your job?) He most certainly understood that, judging from his thunderous expression, and Junko had to find a 'bathroom' very quickly!

---

[6]   *pachinko* is a Japanese gambling passion, a mixture of pinball and fruit machine, of which I understand nothing whatsoever. *Pachinko* parlours are the noisiest places on the planet. Avoid them!

We found one in a *sushi* restaurant. More raw fish, I was growing fins! This time, however, I could sit on real chairs at a real table and, because she was driving, Junko contented herself with just the one 660ml. bottle of 5.5% ABV Sapporo lager. The journey back to Gifu was quite slow, our visit having taken place on a public holiday, *kodomo no hi*[7] (Children's Day) when families fly highly colourful plastic or paper carp, one for each male member of the family, on poles affixed to the upper eaves of their houses. On the way we crossed the Formula1 circuit at Suzuka in Mie *ken*. F1 is a bit faster than *pachinko* but nowhere near as noisy.

*****

One sunny Sunday morning in late September 2002 I decided to make a trip to Himeji to see the Castle of the White Heron, *shirasagijō*. Because I had worked a good deal of overtime in the summer months, I felt justified in travelling by the Bullet Train and hang the additional expense of a reserved seat! This sleek piece of railway engineering is called the 'bullet train' in English because of the streamlined bullet shape of the early locomotives; the Japanese *shinkansen* merely describes it, rather prosaically, as a 'new trunk line'. This train, which looks for all the world like an aircraft without the wings, whisks you at speeds in the region of 200mph in air-conditioned near silence and passenger-pampering comfort.

---

[7]   5th. May

From Nagoya it takes just two hours to reach Tōkyō and forty minutes to reach Kyōto, depending on the service you take. I travelled on the middle of the range *hikari* (light) which has limited stops. The *kodama* (echo) takes longer because it stops at every *shinkansen* station, and the super-fast *nozomi* (hope) was just a bit beyond my wallet. In the event it took a mere ninety minutes to reach Himeji in Hyogo *ken* on the shores of the Inland Sea, facing the island of Shikoku.

The castle is easily visible from the station, a long, broad, arrow-straight avenue leads you ever closer to what, from a distance, appears to be another standard five-storey castle with interesting roof configurations, the usual upward-sweeping eaves etc.[8]

Look backwards however, to see how far you have walked and the scale of the castle becomes awesome. And you are still only halfway down the avenue. The line of the first defensive moat, which protected the surrounding castle town, began approximately on the site of the present JR station.

Shirasagijō is the largest, and surely the most beautiful, original wooden castle left. Accounts differ as to its origins; some say that a fort was built here in 1333; other scholars claim that the castle was begun in the middle of the sixteenth century. What is known is that the entire complex,

---

[8] Apparently the eaves sweep upwards so that evil spirits or ghosts will slide off the roof as they attempt to climb into the building.

including the moats, was completed in 1609. There are only about half-a-dozen wooden castles, which remain today, World War II having done for the rest, although not always as a result of American bombing. Many castles were destroyed by the Japanese themselves to prevent the proud symbols of their martial legacy from falling into enemy hands, although you are unlikely to find that piece of information in school text books, and, for reasons alluded to earlier, they wouldn't believe it anyway.

In common with all other castles, the approach to the main tower, or keep, is fraught with difficulty if you are unfamiliar with the layout. Three heavily defended moats, bridged in only a couple of places, are the first defence. Once inside the keep area the attacker is faced with a perplexing labyrinth of alleyways defended on both sides by stout roofed walls and garrison buildings through whose gun ports and arrow slits the defenders could deliver a murderous hail of missiles.

All the time the approach to the keep is steadily rising, the paths twisting and turning, leading the attacker down blind alleys. The keep itself is built on a massive, outwardly-curving (from the top down) dry stone platform, no mortar being used in the construction. This platform is possibly some forty meters high and was relatively easy to scale if you were prepared to risk the rocks and boiling water or oil that cascaded down from the trapdoors above.

The keep is constructed in the standard manner, a series of rectangular 'boxes', and each one is a little smaller than the box below, to distribute the weight evenly, rises from the stone platform. The lower floors, being more spacious, would be given over to training areas for the warriors and halls where large councils of war could take place. Very steep, open staircases lead from one level to another, usually only one staircase per level as a further defensive measure, the walls are lined with weapon racks and the internal configuration can be altered via sliding panels. On the very top floor there is a shinto shrine and distant views of the Seto Inland Sea.

The castle grounds contain many other buildings essential to the running of such a massive enterprise, storehouses, accomodation for staff officers, *hatamoto*, barracks and, ominously, the *hara kiri maru*. This is the little open hall were ritual suicide was performed and where the sword and the severed head would be reverently washed in the adjacent well.

All the buildings have white-painted walls and light-grey tiled roofs, and the keep, with its two smaller towers standing side by side, is lavishly finished with many pointed gables and upward-sweeping eaves. There are ponds and gardens, earthen walls over 1000 meters long, a pavilion once occupied by the Princess Sen, the daughter of the second Tokugawa shōgun, and her husband, Honda Tadamasa and a broad, grassy terrace at the southern foot of the mighty platform.

Those creaky old TV shows, *Momo Taro Samurai* and *Abarembo Shōgun* are set round about this period, the Momoyama period, i.e. the early 17th Century.

After visiting the castle I had a leisurely stroll around the charming shopping area, dropping my film in for processing on the way. I picked up the prints an hour later and they came already arranged in an album. Then I went to a tiny *izakaya* for a beer and a plateful of prawns. The other customers were all local and they were intrigued by my presence, especially when I told them, in Kansai dialect, that I couldn't understand Kansai dialect!

That did it! I wasn't allowed to pay for my beer. This place was so very tiny that it didn't have a loo; you had to go to the *pachinko* parlour some twenty-odd meters away and use theirs. Or you could use the wall at the side of the pub, they don't seem to mind that sort of thing in Japan, or if they do, they don't say anything of course.[9]

****

---

[9]   I once saw a gentleman in a business suit relieving himself on the pavement outside Gifu station. He'd obviously just got off the Kirin Ichiban Special.

CHAPTER 7

NIHON RYŌRI

'Can you eat Japanese food?' This is a question most frequently asked of the *gaijin* in restaurants or *izakaya* as you sit confidently wielding a pair of chopsticks and gulping down strands of hot *ramen* whilst making very noisy and very satisfying slurping noises[1].

Or whilst you are dipping *sushi*, fish-side down, into a sauce of soya and *wasabi*, a green variety of horseradish which can ream the oesophagus like a wire brush, and then shoving the whole piece, whatever the size, into your mouth. This is not so much a question directed at finding an answer to what is glaringly obvious, but is more of a statement expressing disbelief and which requires further probing and scrutiny.

The Japanese never rely solely on the evidence of their own eyes where the *gaijin* is concerned. They need a deeper appreciation of the poor creature's psyche, but because they are always so irritatingly polite, they leave half the question unasked, i.e.

'Can you eat Japanese food *without pulling a face and throwing up?*'

I was already fairly familiar with *sushi* and *sashimi* before I even went to Japan for the first time in the year 2000, there being a small choice

---

[1]   It is essential to slurp *ramen* as they are piping hot!

of Japanese restaurants in Brighton, but I wasn't quite prepared for the wide variety on offer. I would frequently have lunch at a small establishment called Nomo's, which is where I met Junko.

For under £4.00 I had the standard set lunch which consisted of a bowl of rice, a bowl of *miso* (bean paste) soup, deep-fried prawns and vegetables in batter -*tempura*- pickles, a small selection of raw fish (usually tuna, yellowtail and octopus) and a cup of *chawanmushi*, a sort of savoury egg custard with *shiitake* mushrooms, small pieces of chicken and seaweed.

All was washed down with a large cup of hot green tea, which was refilled as often as required. Because of my working pattern, lunch was usually a leisurely affair, but I was most impressed at the speed at which the regulars could polish off this mini-feast, especially as I still think that using chopsticks is not the most efficient way to eat rice. Japanese rice is a little sticky, so that helps. You also use chopsticks to eat *miso* soup. Work that one out!

Breakfast at the coffee shop across the little road from my flat was, as already mentioned, cheap and satisfying. It never varied and consisted of the drink of your choice (coffee was my choice) a large slice of buttered toast, a small bowl of salad, *sarada*, five deep-fried, sweet dumplings, *dango*, on a wooden skewer and dribbled with maple syrup, a cup of *chawanmushi* and as many glasses of iced water as you required. If you bought a strip of ten tokens the price was even lower. All coffee shops operated this system. Another favourite place for breakfast was Milton Banana which was close to my original flat in Kashima-chō. It offered toast, hard boiled egg, fruit salad or an item of fruit and the inevitable river of iced water.

Alternatively I could cross the Beltway and have a cheap, traditional Japanese breakfast at an establishment called 'Myway'. This consisted of rice, *miso* soup, pickles, grilled fish (salmon or mackerel) and very thin squares of toasted *nori*, which is the same seaweed product that is wrapped around rolled *sushi*. Served with green tea, of course. I had lunch in 'Myway' now and again, and on one occasion the main dish was fried baby green peppers stuffed with minced pork and ginger. It was delicious.

When I was a student and living in the eastern suburbs of Paris I would often attempt to reproduce dishes that I had enjoyed in restaurants, friends' homes and even the school canteen[2], and so it was in Japan. I carefully studied Okawa *kun*'s every move behind the counter in *yoro no taki*, I bought a rice-cooker and a few culinary bits and bobs from the 100-yen shop to complete my *batterie de cuisine*, and set off on the hunt for ingredients.

Have you ever cast your eyes over the vegetable section in a Japanese supermarket? Not the standard onions, carrots and potatoes bit, but the rest? Well it's a bit like trying to read the labels on

---

[2] This canteen was heavily subsidised by the local Communist council and was a gourmet's paradise.

the packaged stuff; you haven't got a clue what you are looking at.

There are long, thin pieces of muddy-looking wood, there are virulent green hand-grenades, there are some limp-looking black things, there are curious white marrow-like objects as hard as concrete and creamy cones of something in sealed bags of water. The helpful price tickets tell you what they are, but, of course, they are written in a combination of *kanji* and *hiragana*.

There was nothing for it, I had to learn *hiragana* at least, and it didn't really take too long, so I was soon in the happy situation of discovering that the muddy wood had an appositely unappetising name, to whit: *gobbo*. It turns out to be burdock and my advice is not to bother with it unless, as a child, you were an incurable chewer of pencils. The white concrete, however, is *daikon*, a Japanese radish which you have shredded raw with *sashimi* or slowly cooked in *miso* and which, so prepared, tastes rather like turnip.

In the event my first attempt at an authentic Japanese meal didn't turn out too badly: raw tuna with *daikon* (OK, bought ready prepared from the supermarket, but the checkout lady was most impressed) grilled marinated chicken - *yaki tori*-boiled rice, *miso* soup and a generous amount of *warm saké*. Subsequent authentic Japanese meals included spaghetti bolognaise and chilli con carne, very popular according to the menus displayed in many restaurants.

Not only are menus displayed, the dishes, in wax replica form, are also on show, a sort of gastronomic Madame Tussaud's which makes choosing a meal easier, especially for the Westerner: 'I'll go for that one, minus the dust *kudasai*!' One restaurant in Ōgaki had a display so ancient that most of the tempting sauces appeared to be greyish-brown and the squid rings were beyond description. The real stuff was all right, though.

What I really recommend everyone to get is a rice cooker. Once I'd got used to mine (via trial and error, the instructions were not immediately clear!) I was producing not only boiled rice but also biriyani-style dishes and a pretty acceptable paella. So you know what to put on your wedding or Christmas list, and make sure it has a programmable timer. Do not get a friend to bring one back from Japan, the voltage is different and the plug won't fit into our sockets.

If you like grated raw cabbage[3], Japan is the place for you. Mountains of it are served with many dishes and the *aficionado* usually sprinkles it liberally with *komi* sauce, a condiment similar to Worcestershire sauce, or with mayonnaise dispensed from a squirty bottle. *Tonkatsu*, fried pork cutlets in breadcrumbs, was a favourite of mine and, served, as it was, with rice, soup, pickles and a green mountain of cabbage, helped to pass the time.

Meiho ham was another natural target for the cabbage industry, as was just about anything that

---

[3] It isn't really grated; it is cut finely, *sengiri* style, into strips.

proclaimed to be accompanied by '*sarada*'. If you are lucky you also get bits of grated raw carrot in *sarada*.

The mighty cabbage, however, assumes an altogether more pivotal rôle in the very popular *okonomiyaki*, a sort of pancake cooked on a flat hotplate and whose principal ingredient is, well, grated cabbage of course. Let's be honest; would *you* eat it as it comes, but boiled?

The noble *brassica* is mixed with flour, eggs and grated yam[4] to make a batter, to which may be added thinly sliced beef, fish or prawns, fried on the hotplate and garnished with chopped spring onions, *benishoga* (pickled red ginger) and dried bonito flakes. It is also added to *yaki-soba*, fried soft noodles with onions, a few beansprouts and soya sauce.

Great favourites in the 'gobble and go' sort of eateries that grace all shopping malls are *kare-raisu*, the Japanese form of curry, and noodles of every description. I used to make curry fairly frequently because it is so easy to do and can be left to come home to after work. All you do is slow cook a few vegetables and some meat or fish, if you want, and add a cube from a block of 'magic curry ingredient'.

This comes in a packet, on which is shown the relative strength of the contents, and it looks like a thick slab of chocolate. This both imparts flavour and thickens the sauce. Serve on an oval dish with the curry up one end and the rice down the

---

[4] This *is* grated.

other, strategically place a few pieces of *benishoga* where the two armies meet and eat with a spoon.

Alternatively you can decide upon *kare-udon*, which is a <u>large</u> bowl of chunky curry-flavoured soup with long, thick wheat noodles in it. This you eat with chopsticks *and* a spoon. Do not forget to slurp, or you'll scald your lips, and try not to wear any of this delicacy on either your face or your clothes.

Many Japanese dishes are really very simple. Take, for example, the delicious *hyaiyakku*, which is just cubes of *tofu* dribbled with soya sauce and topped with grated ginger, dried bonito flakes (*katsobushi*) and very thinly-sliced raw *negi*, long, thin leeks which are added to garnish many dishes, including *miso* soup and *chawanmushi*. A colleague once had a visitor from Tokyo and we all went out for a drink and a bite to eat. She had never heard of *chawanmushi*, but she tried some and she loved it, so there!

I think I enjoyed most of what I ate in Japan, even the food I had in hospital. In fact it was jolly good, especially the 'creamy cones' which, it transpires, are *takenoko*, fresh bamboo shoots and taste superb. At least it was prepared on the premises and only had four floors to travel up to my ward, whereas the bilge I was supposed to eat, years ago, in a Brighton hospital started its journey in Wales! I do not recommend the omelette.

*****

There were some things, however, that were not to my taste, even though I valiantly tried to be appreciative.

One item was *konnyaku*, a substance which looks like kids' party jelly before it is dissolved, except that it is brown, grey, grey-with-black-flecks or near-black. It is lovingly made by what is obviously a very long and complicated process in remote and arcane country locations known only to millions of television viewers, which explains how I know all about this. It is a product of the Devil's Tongue plant and is sold in slabs about the size of those blocks of curry, and is either cubed or cut into strips like slimy rubber bands.

There is little taste and it takes ages to chew, which is why people in the know (like me...now!) swallow it without chewing, rather in the manner of those pretentious clots who think they know how to eat a freshly opened oyster. This delicacy, like *daikon,* is, in my view, best eaten when slowly cooked in *miso*.

Another dubious treat was thin slices of raw horsemeat, which are dipped in a dressing of soya sauce and sesame oil. It has a similar texture to liver just that split second before you cook it. This delicacy is, in my view, best eaten by someone else.

Yet another horror was *uni*, which is the roe of the sea urchin. It has the colour, texture and consistency of what may be euphemistically described as 'semi-digested recycled marine matter' and is, in my view, best eaten by the household pet. And I adore fresh, red tuna, but either raw or cooked right through in a sauce *à la basquaise.* Half-and-half is pretty gross.

Small fish like sardines and *sanma*, a sort of sea-pike, are grilled with their innards still intact. It's fun sorting through the bones and sludge with your trusty chopsticks. As for deep-fried chicken kneecaps, or some such avian cartilage, or stir-fried pig's intestine[5], well, you can have too much of a good thing!

It isn't strictly necessary to eat Japanese style in Japan. There are many western-style eateries: the obvious burger and pizza places, foreign, particularly Italian or Italian-influenced, restaurants. There are 'Irish' pubs (they serve Guinness, the owner once got a postcard from a pal who went to Dubrin and the chef can peel potatoes) steak houses and snackeries like Mr Donut, Vie de France and Café Criel. But why go all the way to Arizona and just look at a builder's trench? Although, having said that, I did once have a huge and very rare steak in a place called 'Bronco Billy'. It was heavenly.

If you are, as I was, mainly self-catering, you could stick to a completely western diet without the roasts. The only ovens I saw were microwaves and I've only used one a couple of times at work in the UK to heat up a pasty, but where's the sense of adventure? Does it stop at the kitchen door? And you have the neighbours to consider. Would *you*

---

[5] Actually I really enjoy this, but only when filled with sausage meat and served with mash.

Marcus Grant

inflict boiled cabbage on *their* nostrils? I once saw a sign in a cheap, residential hotel in Nagoya. It said, 'Please do not cook with a bad smell.'

Again, in Nagoya, there is a super shopping mall called Ōsu where you can get real Turkish döner kebabs and whole spit-roast chickens from a Brazilian café. These are sources of macabre fascination for the locals, who have rarely seen a piece of meat bigger than a small steak.

Of course it isn't just about eating, this food business. There is the whole surrounding culture and ambiance which, like the food itself, can be a delight or a nightmare. The Japanese are noted for their fastidiousness and personal hygiene, so it remains ever a mystery what malignant force created the '*izakaya* from Hell'.

Most restaurants close around 10.00 pm in the city centres and main suburban areas, but many *izkaya* remain open until well into the early hours of the morning, as they don't open until 5.00 pm or later. You know when a place is open because of the orange light, rather like those on a breakdown truck, that rotates outside. They are usually small establishments owned and run by a husband and wife team, serve a limited range of home-cooked food and have a bar with high seats for the customers as well as the usual, often *tatami*, seating area for groups. The husband is always referred to as 'Masta', the wife as 'Mama'.

The walls and ceiling are decorated with the usual knick-knacks; paper lanterns in abundance, various wooden carvings, famous views, posters of popular singers, sportsmen etc. and they are fairly noisy, friendly places where sport and politics are discussed at increasingly befuddled volume. If there's a *karaoke* machine you are guaranteed to be serenaded by an elderly regular of either sex who will invariably demand to know your country, age and blood group. If you are male and single (well, on your own) it could really be your lucky night as the middle-aged lady sitting next to you displays a close manual interest in your thigh.

Such was the *izakaya* near Junko's place. It was entered through traditional sliding wooden doors over which hung a traditional short, panelled curtain of heavy cotton. (This is called a *noren* and it usually bears the name of the establishment. I managed to scrounge one when they closed down *yoro no taki* in February 2003.)[6]

Masta's beaming face bellowed the usual greeting and you were made welcome. So far, so good. You settled down on a seat, ordered a drink, and then it hit you. This place would have reduced a British health and safety official to a prolonged and uncontrollable fit of hysterical laughter and it would be ages before he could regain the necessary strength to sign the closure order.

The gas hob behind the counter, and the tiled backdrop, were both caked in a layer of black grease that must have been there for decades. Puddles of

---

[6]   Yes, they closed it down. This was a heavy blow.

111

old cooking-oil adorned the working-surface. Fat hung in little stalactites from the edge. Cooking utensils showed undeniable evidence of flame-damage. There were almost as many sticky traps for cockroaches as there were paper lanterns and I wasn't entirely sure if they weren't moving. And this was the place where I'd eaten the horsemeat! No wonder it tasted rank!

Then the worst happened. As I was contemplating paying up and getting out, the most enormous rat[7] I have ever been close to sauntered amongst the pots and pans on the floor behind the counter. It was almost cat-sized. I attracted Masta's attention to this revolting rodent.

'Ah yes. It comes every night. I can't seem to get rid of it.' was the mournful response.

'Does it eat horsemeat?' I asked without much hope.

I have been in similar pubs, like the one near the Satō's home in Chita which boasted a rather gruesome kitchen area, but none quite as terminal as this one. The attraction is that the food in these little places is really delicious and quite reasonably priced, and the welcome is usually open and genuine, although some people refuse to believe that foreigners can speak any Japanese at all,

[7]   The word for 'rat' and 'mouse' is the same in Japanese, *nezumi*. A student once told me he had seen 'a big mouse' on a visit to Cambridge.

like Mr Leaflet. Funnily enough they understand perfectly well when you order something that you will ultimately pay hard cash for.

Not a bad idea for a lunch out is the top floor, or basement, depending on where the restaurant area is, of any large department store. A regular jaunt, about once a month, was to one of the restaurants on the 11th floor of Takashima-*ya* in the centre of Gifu city.

I always sat by the window to enjoy the panorama over the Nagara River and views of the nearby pointy hills. I always tried to pick out my block of flats, but never managed to, and I always had the same dish because it was so well cooked and so beautifully presented.

This was *unagi-don*, grilled eel on a bed of savoury, slightly nutty rice, served in a black lacquered oblong box with a lid and accompanied by a delicately flavoured, clear fish soup with a nice bit of eel liver in it, pickled vegetables, a flask of *saké* and the inevitable restorative green tea. All for about a fiver!

One day I was treated to something really special. Just to the north of the Nagara River, on the opposite bank to Kinka *san* is an exquisite hidden valley with a pond, a waterfall and a very old thatched *gassho* with a steeply pitched roof like the ones at Shirakawago. This is now a restaurant, but retains its farmhouse character and appearance.

We sat on the *tatami* floor in a private room overlooking the pond and enjoyed a meal, the majority of the ingredients of which had been gleaned from the little valley. We had deep-fried flower heads in a light *tempura* batter, salads of various plants and herbs, *ayu* (innards intact!) from the river and fresh raw koi carp, *sashimi* style, from the pond. And rice, of course, topped with a raw egg. The tea was prepared from nuts and had a slightly smoky flavour. The whole experience was somehow strangely poetic.

Barbecues are always fun and I went to quite a number, usually near the river, on special occasions such as *hanami*, the cherry-blossom viewing, or just for Sunday enjoyment in the summer, once the rainy season had finished. There was the usual fish and skewered beef, chicken or pork, grilled sweet corn and sweet potatoes, and *yaki-soba* cooked on a flat iron plate placed on the barbecue grill...so easy!

In fact you can enjoy a barbecue at any time of the year, there are countless *yaki niku ya*, indoor grills, where you sit around a table, sunk into the centre of which is a gas barbie, order the raw ingredients from the menu and do-it-yourself. Extractor fans mounted in the ceiling above the table ensure a comfortable experience. Make sure you order *kimuchi* to go with it, a fiery Korean concoction of pickled cabbage and red chillies. You won't be disappointed!

Yakiniku Sakai is a big chain restaurant and a safe place to start because the menu is adequately illustrated and therefore *gaijin*-friendly, all one has to do is smile and point.

There are places which specialize in just one item, like the *omeraisu* restaurant at Gifu station, which only serves rice topped with omelette, albeit a very wide range of omelettes is on offer.

But the most challenging item I tried was *fugu*, the notorious puffer fish which can prove fatal if not prepared properly, i.e. by having every trace of a blood vessel removed before serving. Despite its fearsome reputation it is remarkably bland, and it is estimated that there are only about 250 deaths a year occasioned by consuming this very Japanese speciality, which, out of a population of about 120 million makes it far safer than crossing the road or smoking in bed.

Chilled noodles in summer, hearty meals like *suki-yaki* in winter, regional dishes like *hōtō,* a sort of vegetable stew from Yamanashi, fish and seafood of all shapes and sizes, textures and flavours, the range of Japanese food is as vast as it is varied. I have but scraped the surface in this little chapter. But one thing is certain, I lost five kilos in weight during my time in Japan and I haven't regained much since my return, simply by cutting down on meat, eating oily fish and drinking that wonderful, rejuvenating and life-preserving herb, *ocha*.

****

115

CHAPTER 8

IROIRO

My bike got nicked! Or should I say 'borrowed'? Nobody steals anything in Japan and the two main objects of the borrowers' attention are umbrellas and bicycles. Thus it was, upon my return from work one night, that I discovered that my beloved Granny bike had disappeared from its usual position, chained to the cycle-park railings outside Nishi Gifu station.

Forlornly I walked to *yoro no taki* where I bewailed my misfortune to Ayu *tenchō*. She was sympathetic and offered to give me a bike that had been propped up in the alleyway behind the pub for weeks. It was a smart affair, or would have been with decent tyres and a good clean up, but as it had no mudguards and no basket, it wasn't much use for riding in the rain or for shopping.

I thanked her but declined the offer. I sentimentally showed her the guarantee - cum - I.D. of the missing machine   and she noticed a fascinating clause in the document. Apparently if your bicycle is 'borrowed' within a year of the initial purchase and you report the loss to the police, you get a replacement, free of charge, from the original dealer. There was a police box, a *kōban*, not far away. Next day I was mobile again.

A couple of months later I got a postcard from the police. Thanks to the dealer's sticker on the rear mudguard, they'd found my bike!

When I first arrived in the country I possessed neither bicycle nor umbrella. About a year later I was the proud owner of two bicycles and a number of umbrellas. I think at one point there were five of the things cluttering up my tiny entrance hall, not one of which I had 'borrowed', but which had been lent to me by various coffee-shop proprietors or Mamas when I had been caught out by the odd unforecasted downpour. I remember returning one and then having to borrow it again immediately, and, yes, I mean borrow, not 'borrow'.

The Japanese are wonderfully skilful cyclists. They can squeeze in between fellow pavement users at dizzying speeds, they can ride one-handed in the rain whilst clutching an umbrella, and the (usually) older ladies, ever mindful of the harmful rays of the sun, and ever anxious to maintain a pale complexion, ride holding an umbrella or parasol, even in cloudy conditions and even in covered shopping malls.

I attempted to ride thus without much success and had to wear a waterproof hat or risk getting wet. Because my bike looked exactly like almost every other bike, it was sometimes a problem finding it in the seemingly endless rows of bicycles outside the station or in the town centre shopping arcades.

The problem was easily solved; I affixed a yellow bell, thus allowing instant identification from a distance.

*****

The 'borrowed bike' incident was my first experience of dealing with the police. The second occurred as I was walking to the station one bitterly cold February day to get the train to work. A cruising squad car tailed me for a bit, drove round the block, approached me from the front and the two combat fatigues clad occupants got out.

One was tall, bespectacled and wearing a white facemask to keep his hay fever to himself[1] and the other was about my lack of height and very chatty. Facemask asked me questions about my name, job, where I lived etc., whilst the chummy one jocularly complained about the cold and complimented me on my Japanese language ability. In the event it was just a routine check because I didn't look Japanese enough, they saluted smartly, bowed a bit, and off they went.

There was one occasion when, apparently, I did look Japanese enough. It was on a Saturday evening, I had finished work and, suited, booted and briefcased, I hailed a taxi to take me to the municipal hospital. No, no I was fine; it's just that Junko's bar was right next door to the *shimin byōin*. The rear door opened automatically (they also close automatically, and, if you haven't got the fare, you are locked in until the driver can reach a

---

[1] In Japan they refer to it as 'cedar-fever' because of the effects of planting millions of fast-growing, non-native, cedar trees after WWII in order to replenish the vital stock of wood necessary for house-building. Another triumph for Uncle Sam!

police box) and in I got, settled against the twee antimacassars which embellish all taxis and many private cars, and affixed a thoughtful frown.

Not wishing to engage in a one-way conversation, I extracted, from my briefcase, the first piece of paper that came to hand and pretended to read it. Upon arrival at the hospital I duly paid the fare[2] and made my automatically assisted exit. 'Thank you, doctor,' said the cabbie, and he wasn't being ironic!

Whilst on the subject of emergency services, I taught a student who was an auxiliary fire fighter. He was thirty-ish, well built and, naturally, very fit. He was a member of one of the local mobile shrine-pulling teams, *à la* Takayama. He told me that his hobby, when he could fit it in between his day job in an office, learning English, fire-fighting and all that that job entails, and getting a few short hours' kip in between, was hiking in the big pointy hills behind Ibuki *san*.

One day he was striding out, alone in the forest, when a family of wild boar crossed the path just feet ahead of him. He froze, he told me, totally scared out of his mind. He couldn't even move to shin up a tree. As luck would have it, the family of potential killers ignored his presence and disappeared into the forest.

I found his self-deprecation refreshingly honest and very similar in tone to the simple matter-of-factness characteristic of a British fire fighter of my

---

[2]   A serious word of advice. Never offer a tip to anyone. It is an insult.

acquaintance. Disaster could strike at any moment, but you just get on with things, like mucking in with the lads and pulling half-a-ton of shrine to unwind.

This shrine-pulling stuff is a feature all over the country. The Ōgaki *matsuri* takes place over two days in early summer and stars about a dozen teams of young men who pull and manoeuvre heavy wooden floats around the main streets of the city. All the floats are colourfully decorated and incorporate large figurines and even kimono-clad little girls dancing to *koto* music played on a sound system concealed within the body of the float.

As there are no brakes or steering mechanism on these juggernauts, the process of negotiating corners and inclines is complex and the iron-shod wooden wheels leave their impression on the tarmac.

Each team wears its distinctive uniform of *happi*, a colourful wrap-over cotton jacket worn over white shorts, and the team *hachimaki*, or headband, and some are accompanied by traditionally dressed musicians playing the *shakohachi*, the bamboo flute.

In April 2003 I was taken to watch the Gifu *hi-matsuri*, the fire festival, which involves teams of young men carrying portable shrines, *mikoshi*, on their collective shoulders. This is a most demanding task as the festival parades around the streets for most of the afternoon until assembling in a little park at dusk, after which there is a firework display.

These *mikoshi* are not light, and in one particular festival, in another area of Japan, the rival teams try to knock down each others' shrines, which sounds like madness to me, having seen the things up close. Still I suppose it isn't surprising in a country where, in the depths of winter, hundreds of near-naked men splash about in icy water, as they do during another festival in Gifu city.

It is a point of honour to take part in these events and entry is restricted to the first-born son of the family. Junko's son-in-law, Hiroaki, was in the Gifu fire festival. Whilst he was heaving and straining on his *mikoshi*, I was in the process of cadging a rather fetching, *kanji*-embellished headband from a rival team, who represented the 'powerful hand' shrine, according to the *kanji*.

*****

Not so much a festival but more of a tradition is *hanami*, cherry-blossom viewing. In spring, as well as the weather forecast, there is the cherry-blossom forecast, and many retired people follow the progress of the blossom the length of Japan.

One fine day in March I was strolling along the Gifu *tōzaidori* when Junko pulled up in her car.

'Jump in,' she said and I did.

'Where are we going?' I asked.

'*Hanami*', she replied and, after a brief stop at my flat to pick up my camera, we drove to a spot near the Nagara River where there was a modern reproduction of an old Nobunaga castle, *ichiya-jo*, and a splendid display of blossom.

We strolled alongside a small river, the *saigawa*, which flows parallel to the *nagaragawa*, under a swathe of heavy blossoms. It was like being in a translucent, pink tunnel. We bought a couple of *bento* boxes and enjoyed a leisurely lunch under the trees at the foot of the castle.

Thereafter we visited Junko's family grave, where she said a little prayer. Japanese graves are like obelisks mounted on a plinth, and what at first sight appears to be an urn is, in fact, the handles of sliding doors, behind which is a pit to contain the family ashes.

That's how I met Junko's mum, a small portion of whom still had a piece of kimono attached.

*****

Some western traditions have caught on in Japan, notably Valentine's Day, when ladies offer gifts of chocolate to gentlemen to whom they take a shine. I received many gifts of chocolate...they really do take this *giri* business seriously! There are no such things as Valentine cards, and as this is a women's thing the men don't have much of a part to play; until the following month when White Day falls on the 14th. That is when the gentlemen reciprocate the gifts of chocolate that have been bestowed on them, and that is definitely a case of *giri*!

Another western festival that the Japanese pay lip service to is Christmas. From the latter part of November shopping malls and department stores are heaving with Santa Clauses, Christmas trees, lights and baubles, fairies and all the concomitant trappings of a good, old fashioned, sickly sentimental Disney Christmas.

The great day arrives and everybody goes to work as usual. Japan is a Buddhist society, so New Year is the big one. December 23rd is a national holiday, however, that day being the Emperor's birthday.

I visited shrines occasionally to say a little prayer for my family back home, and once I took an Australian couple to Ōsu Kannon, a large shrine in Nagoya. These people were about my age and were practising Christians, although they didn't shove it down your throat. I went through the motions, the hand washing, the incense bit and the ringing of the bell. I waggled the rope and the bell (actually it was a gong) went 'bonk bonk'. Mr Aussie said, 'That's not very loud.' 'Ah,' said I, 'but God can hear it!' Mr Aussie gave a weak smile.

There is a most graphic festival in the not-too-distant Komaki city, in Aichi *ken*, on March 15th. Throughout the year a small team of highly skilled woodcarvers works on the production of an anatomically accurate and highly polished giant phallus, which is paraded through the streets and, finally, reverently placed in the Tagata shrine.

It is accompanied on its journey by crowds of people, mainly women, clutching smaller, but nonetheless sizeable, wooden willies to ensure fertility. I saw this on telly and I sympathised with the rather bashful young American couple who were being interviewed during the parade. No matter how remote the location, how brief the clip, how long ago the event was immortalised, if you're on the box it's a dead certainty that, somehow, one of your mates will spot you.

I worked with a Japanese teacher of English who quite readily informed me that he had visited the shrine to stroke the phallus in order to guarantee procreation, but as far as I knew it hadn't worked up until that point. Oh, and he took his wife along to make doubly sure. What a touching picture that conjures up. I couldn't even get my wife to come along and watch me play Rugby after we were married.

*****

She certainly wouldn't have been seen dead with me on my 56th birthday. On that day Junko presented me with a full set of traditional *wafuku*, Japanese clothing, which had belonged to her father, a very sprightly 77 year-old. He would occasionally nip off somewhere, such as China, with a few pals to have a laddish few days away and to stock up on even cheaper ciggies. He, it seems, had a large wardrobe of traditional clothes, some unworn, so he was glad to unload a few pieces.

There was a blue silk under-kimono, decorated with Japanese motifs and having a plain, darker blue, shawl collar. This would be visible under the kimono proper, a garment of high quality bluish-grey wool which was held together by a dark blue silk *obi*, a wide 'belt' about three metres long which is worn round the hips, not the waist. That's how women wear an *obi*.

On top of this is worn a matching jacket, a *haori*, open at the front but held together by a decorative *himo*, a tassled short length of cord. On my feet I wore *tabi*, split-toed brilliant-white sort of socks with a stiffened sole, and a pair of *geta*, wooden flip-flops with raised platforms. With my antique folding fan (not the Kyōto one, this was another present from Junko's dad's collection) stuck into my *obi* I was ready to hit the bright lights.

Well, almost. It's the Devil's own job to get into this gear, both kimono and the jacket having large, square sleeves which must be successively tucked into each other. And the two kimono must be secured by narrow cotton belts before the *obi* is tied - naturally in a particular way. There are no buttons or hooks, except for affixing the *himo* and for fastening the *tabi*.

My birthday falls a couple of months before Christmas and, as I was scheduled to work on Christmas Day that year, I decided to wear my best clothes, i.e. the *wafuku*, for the occasion. I had time to practice getting in to it, and on the great day I donned my glad rags and swaggered my way to the station.

It's strange, wearing this stuff makes you adopt a haughty *samurai* swagger; maybe because it's so damned tight! I had a little cloth bag for my essentials - keys, wallet, reading specs, ciggies, lighter - just like *Momo Taro*, and I felt rather splendid. Nobody turned a hair or raised an eyebrow as I made my stately progress to work.

My colleagues and students, all Japanese, were knocked out by my elegance. 'Did you wear that by yourself?' asked a stunned Nozomi, meaning 'did I put it on unaided.' 'Well, yes,' I replied, 'There's no-one else in here.'

After work I went to my usual after-work-on-Saturdays-with-Cameron *izakaya*, a sweet little wood-panelled place called *teppen* (mountain summit) whose Masta and Mama had adopted both Cam and me. Cam was married to a Japanese lady, Keiko, who produced a son, coincidentally on my wife's birthday, and Mama took genuine pleasure in this new arrival.

She cooed over the photos and it became an ongoing game to determine which parent young Jonah resembled *this* week as the months rolled by and as the photos rolled in. They were also very taken with a couple of photos of my daughter which Masta immediately dashed out to colour copy at the nearest *kombini*. They were always kept to hand behind the bar. Well, she <u>is</u> a looker!

They were thrilled to see me in my *wafuku*, Mama, especially, being a bit conservative. I was assured that I looked just right and that the clothing was of a really high quality. These were lovely people. At one stage they gave me a present, a *saké* set consisting of four blue and white cups and two matching flasks.

Anyway, after a couple of beers I went to take Junko her Christmas present, a large, earthenware stew pot, because she didn't have one[3]. Her present to me was some more old stuff from the family house in the nearby town of Hozumi, specifically an antique *saké* set of exquisite porcelain in a plain wooden box inscribed with *kanji* so old that not even the traditionally-minded, cultivated Junko could decipher some of the characters. I was constantly deeply moved by the sheer kindness of people and I tried to reciprocate in as appropriate a way as I could.

When I first moved into my flat I had nothing on the walls to look at. I remedied this by buying a poster of Gifu castle as it had looked during the Nobunaga period, then, after a little browse round the 100 yen shop, I suddenly had an idea for another kind of decoration.

They sold bamboo blinds, *sudare*, about 80cms. long by 45cms. wide. I just happened to have stencils of the *kanji* for 'earth', 'fire', 'wind'

---

[3] She had a large aluminium saucepan, but a winter favourite, *kaki nabe*, oyster stew, tastes much better cooked in earthenware, as does *houtou* and other slowly cooked dishes.

and 'water', gleaned from a lifestyle magazine in the UK, so I bought some black ink and produced a rather natty *makimono*, a decorative scroll. I painted my *inkan* in red in the bottom corner and there we were, an instant wall hanging for about £1.75.

I'd really hit on something here, cheap presents, light enough to put in a suitcase and take with me on my scheduled trip home for a couple of weeks in August, so I duly churned out a few more. Teppen's interior, as stated, was all wood panelling and built single-handedly by Masta. There was an alcove with a space just crying out for a homemade, bamboo *makimono*. With great ceremony I presented one to Mama; it was hung up immediately and was given pride of place in the *izakaya*. I would henceforth be identified to all and sundry as its creator each time I made my after-work pilgrimage.

I had a bash at learning another skill, *chigiri-e*, the Japanese art of producing pictures, a little like collages, from torn pieces of *washi*, a Japanese variety of paper. I had begun taking Japanese language lessons in a study/meeting complex at Gifu station. The teachers were all volunteers, the lessons were about £1 for 90 minutes and helped me to succeed in the Japanese Language Proficiency Test, admittedly at lower intermediate level. One of the teachers was also an accomplished *chigiri-e* artist and held a workshop for the students of Japanese.

After a couple of hours' wrestling with templates and tearing small pieces of *washi* into the right shape, I managed to produce a pleasing composition which depicted two cranes in flight. This was something else to adorn my wall and which complemented a *chigiri-e* cum *origami* composition made by one of my students, Keiko *san*, and which was a beautiful little work depicting an Emperor and Empress from the Heian era, the time of Murasaki. Traditionally the faces are plain white, without features, and these looked three-dimensional. 'How did you do that?' I asked in admiration.

'Oh, it's quite easy,' came the reply, 'They're cotton buds!'

My flat was rapidly turning into an art gallery. As well as the *makimono* and the *chigiri-e* on the walls, my bookcase was adorned with a *byōbu*, a folding, six-panelled screen depicting the battle of Sekigahara. There was an enlargement of a photo I'd taken of Himeji castle and various other assorted bric-à-brac, such as a paper lantern, a reproduction print of a *samurai* and a shrine-arrow, a New Year's gift from Kazumi.

I also had a display case of five quite different, individually crafted *choko*, *saké* cups, each of which contains some real gold, and which was a present from a group of five adult students whom I had taught throughout my first year there. I named each *choko* after each student: Mayuko, Yoshiko, Kumi, Rie and Shigeto, and even placed the cups in the same order as the students had chosen to sit. I look at the cups now and I see their faces, I hear their voices, I correct their English.

To give a more 'Japanese' feel to my flat, I put down a couple of lengths of *tatami* floor covering across the centre of the room, both to visually break up the expanse of wood flooring and to define my eating/sitting/sleeping area. I had a sofa bed which hugged the floor, and for visitors I had traditional floor cushions, *zabuton*, and an easy chair which also hugged the floor.

This chair could be folded flat and, although a little bulky, it was fairly light and I managed to get it home from the store strapped to the carrier of my trusty bicycle. It could also be turned into a bed and was put to good use one night when Rohan missed the last train back to Ichinomiya. I don't really blame him; if I had been forced to live in Ichinomiya I'd have missed the last train, too, and probably every one before that. I used to refer to the place as 'Ichi-bitchy-fucking-nomiya'. Didn't like it much.

The only interesting feature[4] of Ichinomiya was a shop, just across the main road from the school, which sold fancy unguents and perfumes from overseas. That's not the interesting bit, but the name of this shop was '*kura*' and said so in a large *kanji* above the display window. *Kura* was my *inkan*, my personal seal. I had wanted 'gu-ra', the first two letters of my name if you say it in a

---

[4]   Interesting to *me*, that is.

Japanese manner, but 'gu-ra' didn't exist so I settled for *kura*, which is quite appropriate, because one interpretation of *kura* is gran<u>ary</u>!

I often had great fun eruditely explaining my choice of *inkan*, writing my family name in *katakana*, the writing system used for words of foreign origin, and making the phonetic connection with 'granary'. I hadn't the heart, or the linguistic ability, to tell them the truth until I had learnt the Japanese for 'coincidence'!

Much more of a coincidence occurred after I had taken the Proficiency Test in Nagoya. On the train back to Gifu I encountered another European, who had also just taken the test. He turned out to be French and I jumped at the chance to practise my language skills. Thankfully I hadn't forgotten any of it, despite having no opportunity whatsoever to speak French in my little backwater of Japan. It transpired that he was from Rennes, the first city that I had ever stayed in in France as a teenager on a school exchange. As part of the exchange we were required to attend lessons at the Lycée Châteaubriand. Yes, you've guessed it; we had both been to the same school, half a world away, albeit twenty years apart and albeit, for my part, rather briefly. *Comme le monde est petit.*

****

CHAPTER 9

WA - EI

Everywhere you care to look in Japan you come across the English language. I shall rephrase that. Everywhere you care to look in Japan you come across English words. There is a difference: these words are strung together without any thought of coherence, cohesion or syntax. There is more coherence in *Finnegan's Wake* than on a Japanese sweatshirt. How about this for an example?

'Silence in total feeling, measuring steps to horror in life'

This is fine in terms of syntax, but what on earth does it mean? It might make sense to Bob Dylan or to Edgar Allen Poe, but I'm damned if I can understand it. But then, I don't do magic mushrooms.

Or this?

'It is glory that to all world to love'

Ok. We are getting a more coherent message here, but the syntax is all screwed up. How does this come about? Allow me to attempt an explanation.

These legends are taken at random from a computer bank and regurgitated onto some sort of technological wizardry which will transform them into trendy street wear. I attribute this development to Tony Blair, whose economical use of the English language has been the inspiration for hundreds of Japanese producers of sweatshirts. Try these for size:

'Education, education, education.'

How succinct, how emotive, and how meaningless. Yet it drew ovations from the assembled faithful. And so did this:

'Tough on crime, tough on the causes of crime.'

The pattern is clear. 'Nouns, not verbs.' 'Reduce use of articles.' 'Significant adjectives.' 'Message, not meaning.'

Not surprisingly those masters of imitation, the Japanese, have seized upon this new expressiveness to display to the world their ability to transform and embellish a variety of English which is not to be found in any textbook. A perfect example of this curious usage appeared on a series of TV adverts for a range of skin care products for women.

A matronly figure interviewed various famous female personalities who gushingly extolled the virtues of these unguents. Whilst this lengthy procedure was under way, a string of captions rolled intermittently across the bottom of the screen. They included the following gems:

It is washed properly.

Skin is prepared.

If it is done, it can be done. (Macbeth?)

It keeps running with a sister.

That it glitters a woman are visited. (Prescott?)

What can I say? Either these messages are some form of obscure Zen Buddhist thought processes, or they are just gibberish. I concentrated so much on the captions that I have completely forgotten the name of the product that was being advertised, not that I would have bought it anyway. Apart from the legends that could be read on the plethora of meaningless sweatshirts, these were the most puzzling examples of what I came to refer to as 'Japlish'.

Because of all the English being bandied about, the Japanese suddenly become experts in a field that is mainly a closed book to the majority of the population. However hard one might try, it is very difficult to persuade a Japanese who has a modicum of English that they sometimes get it wrong.

A case in point was when a student, who had a responsible job with a chemical company, came to ask my advice about a checklist of an operational process which involved each member of staff signing their name once they had completed their part of the process. The question was how to head the column.

The student's boss had insisted on the word 'worker'. I said it was acceptable, but that a more usual term, and one I don't particularly like, is 'operative' or, alternatively, 'staff', thus avoiding the slightly pejorative overtone that 'worker' imparts. Back came my student the following Saturday. 'Worker' it was to be.

When you tell a female student that a 'meat shop' is called a 'butcher's' in my country, she looks as if she might faint. Even Mr No Knackers could not be convinced that, whenever he and his friends decided that I would throw a party in my flat, it was just a party, pure and simple, and not a 'home party'. Hey-ho!

I do not intend, in this short chapter, to write reams of examples of Japlish, there are a number of web sites dedicated to this fascinating study. Instead I merely wish to impart a flavour of a phenomenon which is an integral part of Japanese life, as is reflected in their writing systems.

There are many words of English origin used in everyday spoken and written Japanese, the obvious ones being *hamba-ga-*, *takushi* and *basu*, 'ice-cream' is slightly modified to *softo-kureemu,* and a separate writing system, *katakana,* as already mentioned in the previous chapter, is reserved mainly for words of foreign origin. Thus 'bus stop' will be written in two different systems, *basu* being written in *katakana* and *noriba* (stop) in *hiragana,* a cursive script which, like *katakana,* is based on the Japanese syllables.

As previously mentioned, a trip to the supermarket was inspiration enough to learn these two writing systems at least. There is, however, an awful lot of *romaji,* the Roman alphabet, to be seen, which is very helpful at railway stations. It is nice to know where you are.

Whenever I went by train from Nishi Gifu to Headquarters in Nagoya, I was always amused by a large sign on a warehouse which read:

Madras Shoes
Italy

There's nothing at all wrong with the language, of course, but I rather liked the cross-continental flavour of the imagery.

Closer to home, a short walk from my flat, there was a smart little eatery, the owners of which were anxious for the general public not to use their rubbish area, so they promised to grass on them if they did. To this effect they had affixed a hand-written notice to their fence. This was written in both Japanese and 'English'. It read:

Illegal throw will be informed.

I thought this was rather charming and at least the syntax was accurate, if the lexis left something to be desired. What I don't quite understand is why the sign should have been partly written in English. Nishinoshō was hardly teeming with English speakers. Perhaps, like the underpass, it had been placed there for my sole benefit. How thoughtful.

A label that was attached to a purchase I made in Sanshin read, quite simply, 'Nice Garlic' and so it turned out to be. And I frequently bought blocks of 'House Curry', but I never bothered with the 'Stew de Veau'; it sounded as inedible as the 'cheese curry'. The local pharmaceutical superstore was called 'Health Bank' and sold a vast array of medication, beauty products, cleaning materials, booze and ciggies in packs of 1000.

Another food-related legend appeared on the sides of a delivery van which called frequently at the local supermarket. This time it was in English only and bore the following delightful exhortation:

Eat Happy Table Together

Isn't that just a lovely idea? It started me thinking that Japlish could be put to effective use to fill the conviviality gap that, unfortunately, exists in English. What, for example, is the English for *bon appétit* ? There is a cosiness and almost childlike simplicity about this reference to family life. Items such as bed linen are often embellished with comforting imagery, such as 'Cosy Life' and 'Friendly Pillow'. Pencil cases have such things as 'Joyful School' written all over them, and, of course, the most endearing Japanese creation is a sweet little cartoon character and cuddly toy called 'Hello Kitty'. I don't think that 'Hello Kitty' does anything; it just exists, it just sits there on gloves and T-shirts and notepads and lunch boxes and, well, everything really.

The cosiness theme was continued by the name of the area of Gifu station which housed a bookshop, a computer suite and the teaching and function rooms mentioned in Chapter One. This was 'Heartful Square' (written in *katakana*) which included 'Heartful Café' where the coffee was most inexpensive and very good. This place was mainly run by volunteers, people like my Japanese teachers, it provided a wide range of community services and it really lived up to its caring name, even if the word cannot be found in any of my dictionaries.

Japlish is not an invention of mine. Many English-based words are in everyday use. I have already referred to 'last orders'. The breakfast that is offered in coffee shops is called *monning sabis*, is available until midday and, apparently, is to be experienced only in Gifu *ken*. 'Service', *sabis*, is the way of saying 'free offer'. Thus when I had my photos processed I was given a free album to put them in…*sabis*..

The dry cleaners announced itself, in *katakana*, as *kureeningu*. And whenever the *ji-ho-ba witu-nesu* came to call, I would play the same naughty little game that I played with the sweet little NHK man. 'Excuse me. Don't know what you're going on about,' I would screech in an East Brighton accent that not even I could understand.

It is not only the English language that is at risk. The French language is another object of the improvements that the Japanese love to make. The accents that help us to pronounce French correctly, à ç é ë î etc. are probably viewed by the Japanese as some sort of topping, like the hundreds-and-thousands that are sometimes sprinkled on cake icing.

Thus it was that I spotted a fabric shop called 'La Forêt' with the circumflex removed from the letter 'e' and an acute accent balancing precariously on the letter 'r'. Once again, my happiness was complete.

The Germans don't get off lightly either. The Japanese for 'part time work' is *arubaito*. The German for work is 'Arbeit'. Obviously the Japanese think they work harder than the Germans. Well, certainly they work longer hours, but harder?

Another tentative foray into European languages is the otherwise excellent car manufacturer, Toyota's, choice of name for a popular model, the Corolla. The 'r' and the 'l' sounds are the most difficult for the Japanese to produce and there is a different stress on individual syllables, depending on the base meaning of the word. Yes, well, that's fine in Japanese, but would you buy a car which, according to the telly-ads, proudly proclaims to be the 'Toyota Cholera'?

A real buzzword for the Japanese is the word 'my'. The Japanese for 'car' is *kuruma*, but there are still some people who use the slightly outdated expression *mycar*. One of the products of the company I worked for was a programme of conversation lessons entitled 'My Lesson Plan'. The word 'my' imparts a sense of ownership, of something personal and individual that is often lacking in the corporate mind of the average Japanese salaryman. Sanshin supermarket sold a range of cheap fruit drinks called, simply, 'My...' hence 'My Orange', 'My Grapefruit' etc. A tin of this stuff cost a few pence and the quality was really very good. So 'my' tends to reassure people and guarantee a more fulfilled existence, although I do not recall, whilst in hospital, having seen 'My catheter' or 'My intravenous drip'.

The most intriguing motto that I saw, and one which I found increasingly disturbing as I thought about the imagery and implications that it conjured up, was to be found on a flannelette toilet roll holder in Junko's house. The message was: *Juicy Cross*

I will leave you to interpret that one!

It is, of course, easy to mock other nations' use of the English language, especially when one considers that, by and large, the English are such dismal linguists, and the Japanese should be given three cheers for having a go. Having said that I did wonder whether the English language was being used as a means of communication or as a fashion accessory, something brightly coloured and frivolous which served no purpose other than to cheer you up a bit or to make you feel a bit superior. Whatever the answer, it was somehow rather comforting, especially at first, to come across so many English words[1], even if most of them were just meaningless fun.

****

---

[1] It is quite extraordinary how you can board an aircraft being perfectly able to read and write and then get off it functionally illiterate!

CHAPTER 10

SHIGOTO

My primary purpose in going to Japan was to learn the language, but I had to support my family and myself of course. This I did by working for one of the Big Four language institutes, which are conveniently located close to major rail or underground (subway) stations. Usually one works in three different schools during the week. No, I don't know why, this is not the norm in other institutions.

I was scheduled to work in Gifu and Ichinomiya cities, and in the town of Ōgaki,[1] but I did quite a lot of overtime in other schools, some of them in relatively remote locations and some of them well over an hour's train ride away. This meant that, very occasionally, I would not arrive home much before midnight.

The working day was not onerous, just six hours between the hours of 3.30 and 9.30 pm. with two days off per week, one of which was Sunday. I chose Thursday as my other day off, which meant that my week was nicely split into two short bursts of working time. In addition each employee received five paid 'flexi days' which could be taken at almost any time with sufficient notification, two weeks' holiday at New Year, two weeks in August, Golden Week[2] at the end of April/beginning of May and every National Holiday.

---

[1] Ishida Mitsunari made Ōgaki castle his headquarters prior to the battle of Sekigahara in 1600.

[2] There are three national holidays during this period, hence the name Golden Week.

143

This is a very generous package in terms of Japanese working conditions. The salary wasn't bad either and I often worked overtime on Thursdays. And it was nice to get back the travelling expenses which you don't really miss out of a daily budget, but which build up to quite a sum over the period of a month

The job itself was, for the most part, quite enjoyable: a couple of classes for children with a maximum number of eight in the group, followed by conversation classes for adults, maximum of four. This sounds fairly amenable, but when on considers that the 'Kids' classes were fifty minutes or one hour in length, a faint note of horror begins to creep in.

Japanese children are hideously over-indulged and seem to have an alarmingly extended period of infancy. I observed 'lessons' at the first school I went to where the little darlings would be crawling all over the low tables or attempting to inflict a little bit of friendly damage on each other. The mothers, meanwhile, would kneel immobile and expressionless, in total silence, at one end of the room. After the lesson they would shower their offspring with effusive praise.

In my institute the mothers would observe the lessons through large picture windows and the more the kids laughed, the more radiantly the mums would beam. We were told at a training session that Kids' Classes were primarily for fun and if they picked up any English along the way, that was a bonus. We sat on cushions on the floor (naturally with our shoes off) we rolled around, we ran around, we played silly games, we chanted English words and, amazingly, the kids all remembered the previous week's vocabulary.

I do not think, however, that I actually taught very much meaningful language in proportion to the physical and mental effort that I had to put in. I regarded this part of the job as child minding, for which I am less than qualified, although I must admit that most of the older children were nicely behaved and very friendly. Most of the younger ones, particularly the boys, were monsters.

The director of one of the schools I worked in, at 'Ichi-bitchy', did not help much. His idea of making the kids ready for a lesson was to wind them into a frenzy with his peculiar antics, which included picking up and swinging round the smaller ones and rubbing his buttocks into the faces of larger ones. He had a stentorian voice, a gushing manner and irrepressible optimism.

I was late for work one day because the train had been delayed, so I rang ahead to warn the school. I duly arrived with the necessary document which confirmed that the late arrival was not my fault. You need this if you don't want to lose money.

I explained that there had been an earthquake, *jishin*, at which he burst out laughing. He had obviously given JR a call. 'Not *jishin*', he giggled, '*jisatsu*, suicide.' Hilarious! He turned up at Halloween appropriately dressed as a clown and, naturally, he was Santa Claus at Christmas. Eventually he was demoted to a mundane office job in the kids' section at Headquarters and a real director was brought in.

But, as they say, every cloud has a silver lining, and my late arrival that day meant that I missed my least favourite kids' class. I managed to put up with these classes because they took place in the early part of the working day and there were usually just two of them. Indeed, I owe a debt of gratitude to the existence of kids because of the lucrative opportunities for Sunday working that they provided through their summer parties, Halloween parties and annual speaking tests.

There were also occasions when I conducted pronunciation workshops for Japanese teachers of English, and these were great fun. I once worked for twenty-three days without a break and I looked forward to my pay slip at the end of that particular month.

The adult classes were mainly something to look forward to, but sometimes I was a little wary because, like all the other teachers, I was never certain which level I would be given on any particular day or who would be in the group. I did take care to look in the week's diary, but it could change at any time, of course.

The company operated a system of free time lessons, which the students would book in advance according to their availability. As a result I could only count on a regular pattern of attendance for part of most days, except for the days when I had a regular *kyufukin* class.

This was a class for students who were funded by the government to the tune of 80% of their fees as long as they attended 80% of the course and the same students came at the same time once a week. I have already mentioned the beautiful present of *saké* cups that one such class gave me. This meant that one could plan ahead.

Otherwise the classes were English conversation, *ei kaiwa*, which were based on a dire series of mind-numbing textbooks produced by the company. The basic format of the lessons was standard enough, presentation, controlled practice and then production, but the content was very thin and repetetive.

The conversation classes lasted forty minutes and could contain up to four students. As the students were able to choose their topic from the books, they had all completed mostly different units, albeit at the same level. Thus each lesson began with a few minutes negotiation; 'So, everybody, what shall we do today?' (Smile brightly!) Here's a word of advice. Never ask a group of Japanese a direct question, which requires an immediate answer.

A simple question such as, 'How are you?' will result in a group of uniformly non-committal expressions, sagely nodding heads and a collective 'Mm' sound as if agreeing with you. Getting them to decide on a topic of conversation is almost impossible because they are completely baffled by the novelty of having to make an instant decision.

I found that asking questions is a fruitless task and the best way to get a response is to tell the student to do something, so 'Tell me how you are' works better than 'How are you?'

The problem is more intense the more elementary the level of the student. I was fortunate to teach a group of advanced students who didn't like the book either and wanted real English with grammatical explanations as and when required. Although they were part of the free time lesson system, they always booked the same weekly slot together which, because of the timings of the lessons, ensured that they had me to teach them. I was, naturally, very gratified by such a vote of confidence.

We explored idiomatic English, English culture etc. and I was at great pains to point out that I was a speaker of British, not American, English. They appreciated this and they appreciated the fact that I wasn't bothered if they wanted to speak US English, it was just that I wouldn't because it is unnatural for me to attempt it. One student, the professor, was totally flabbergasted to learn that Winnie the Pooh is, in fact, an English creation, not a Disney clone.

Another fairly regular member of the group was a very good English speaker who had his own agenda. He wore the same sort of jacket that Geography teachers are given to wearing, you know, the one that appears to be made out of coconut matting. He would frequently regale us, in

Japanese, with songs of his own composition and would present us with photocopies of the words and music.

He once went missing for a few months. Upon his return he informed us, without the slightest hint of embarrassment, that he had been in a psychiatric hospital. This surprised nobody but I could sense the embarrassment that the group felt on his behalf, not that they showed it. It is *de rigeur* to mask one's true emotions.

*****

A number of my students were still at high school, preparing for their university entrance examinations. The Japanese education system is rigidly examination-based and is highly competitive. Thus, after school, many students go to a private cram school, *juku*, and, as a result, they are totally worn out by the time they get to English conversation classes. This is admirable. They attend an English conversation class because they have very little opportunity to practise their spoken English at regular school.[3]

I have observed Japanese teachers in action. Their method is quite straightforward; they line up a large number of students in serried ranks and shout at them for about an hour, making extensive use of the whiteboard.[4] The only occasional interaction is between teacher and student.

---

[3] I also had a number of university students in my classes for the same reason.

[4] I never saw an OHP in Japan.

In spite of their fatigue and their frustration, these youngsters attend willingly and participate with great enthusiasm, sometimes twice a week, for the novelty of having a chance to chat in English.[5] I once made the mistake of trying to speak to one of these revered pedagogues in Japanese. His response was, 'That is not the way we say this,' and made no indication that he was willing to correct me. Well, thank you, dear colleague.

Imagine, then, the great fun that we had at staff 'parties'. These merry gatherings were usually held in an up-market *izakaya* for a minimum fee of 3000 yen, which included all the drink you could wish for. You had about two hours to do it in. Brilliant! I rarely spent more than 1500 yen for a meal and a couple of drinks in a whole evening in the places I went to.[6] And I didn't have to endure the grinding formality of waiting for the school director to turn up whilst the drink that I had ordered became increasingly unappetising as it sat, untouched, in front of me.

Once the august personage had given the go-ahead, we could swill and guzzle to our hearts' content.

Thereafter we would pretend to get on with each other and would exchange pleasantries until reality kicked in and we all took shelter in our monolingual enclaves. The staff/student parties

---

[5] My Japanese Language Proficiency test had no oral component.

[6] I didn't have to pay a penny in Junko's bar; I was part of the family. Her granddaughter Kanna (aged 2) loved me, once she had got used to my exotic appearance!

towards the end of the year, known as *bo nen kai* (saying goodbye to the fading year) were much more enjoyable because the students made no pretence about speaking English and just got on with having a good time. If their teachers could join in, so much the better. Some of the male students even removed their ties.

*****

Sometimes a student would not arrive for the appointed lesson, which often meant that the teacher had forty minutes free. Not a chance! There was plenty of mundane stuff to do, work which would normally be undertaken by the Japanese office staff, such as folding, stamping, gluing, highlighting and stapling leaflets, but give them the opportunity and they will offload it onto someone else. I can't really blame them; they just haven't got the required space in their very cramped working areas.

Thus I have folded, stamped, glued, highlighted and stapled leaflets between the *tōkaidō* and the *nakasendō* in four prefectures. These leaflets must be sorted into batches of fifty, no more, no less, and are later given to part-time workers who distribute them, on the street outside the school, to the general public.

This is a thankless task as leaflet distributors are almost invisible to the naked eye, so the technique is to extend an arm in order to impede the progress of the passers-by, in the manner of the lovely Mr Leaflet, or to leap out in front of them waving the things.

I was quite amused, upon leaving Ōgaki station on the way to work one day, to be offered a leaflet for a rival company. The young lady also saw the funny side when I told her what my job was.

The office staff are very friendly and amenable on the surface, but in reality they are watching you like hawks and will report any transgressions or deviant behaviour, such as allowing anyone to see your true emotions, as I found out.

I was working overtime in one of the schools in Nagoya and, one student having failed to arrive, I was put on leaflet duty. I soon made little work of four hundred leaflets and presented them, neatly rubber-banded together in batches of exactly fifty, to the staff, whose English was pretty good, on the counter. 'All finished,' I said brightly, 'where do you want me to put them?' No response! Nothing! I was totally blanked. 'Hello,' I said, rather irritated, 'Am I invisible?'

Being a *gaijin* I probably was. The next day I got an ear bashing from personnel. They just wouldn't have it that I was doing them a favour on my day off. Sure, I was getting paid, but give and take just isn't the Japanese way, which in effect meant that I had to be polite, but they didn't.

Mind you, they were on rubbish wages and they worked much longer hours than I did, so they reserved all their grovelling for the customers who, in Japan, are not kings but gods. I have seen them running to answer the phone; three rings are permitted. Four rings are just unacceptable.

But I did get rather shirty on occasions and sometimes thought that it was about time that the Japanese grew up and joined the real world.

No matter, I was treated with politeness and respect by my students and my efforts were met largely with gratitude and appreciation, which made a nice change from years of having to deal with an increasing succession of insult and indifference to my subjects in schools in England.

Initially I had intended to spend one year in Japan, but in fact I stayed for two and a half years, popping back to the UK for my August holiday for a couple of weeks each year. This, I recognise, was rather selfish of me, but I was determined to achieve a decent level of conversational language. I also found that coming back to my home town, a very Japanese custom in the month of August, involved serious culture shock.

I had forgotten about the semi-naked, tattooed hordes of aggressive barbarian males that roam the streets guzzling cans of lager. I had forgotten about the touching way in which some simple folk leave offerings of old fridges and washing machines to the *kami* of their front garden, or decorate their trees with supermarket carrier bags. I wasn't particularly looking forward to returning to all that.

Another factor was that I had a job in Japan and the thought of applying for work all over again, especially at my age, was something I was anxious to defer. In the event I needn't have worried, I found a job within a week of my ultimate return.

I had had some wonderful experiences in Japan. I had tried to live as close to Japanese society as my background and linguistic limitations would allow, and I think that I was extremely fortunate to have been admitted to a number of circles; the coffee shop, the pub *yoro no taki* and the Kuwano family.

I owe a great debt of gratitude to Nonaka *san* for befriending me and to Junko *chan* for giving me valuable insights into the Japanese way.

I never quite got the hang of sitting cross-legged on cushions on the floor when eating, but I did at one stage find myself bowing as I was speaking on the phone. It was time to go home!

****

Lightning Source UK Ltd.
Milton Keynes UK
UKOW040852210513

211007UK00001B/9/A